THE
ARCHERS
Quizbook

THE
ARCHERS
Quizbook

Join Ambridge treasure Lynda Snell
on a quiz quest around Britain's
most loved village

Quizzes by The Puzzle House
Introductions by Caroline Harrington

WEIDENFELD & NICOLSON

First published in Great Britain in 2020 by Weidenfeld & Nicolson
an imprint of The Orion Publishing Group Ltd
Carmelite House, 50 Victoria Embankment
London EC4Y 0DZ

An Hachette UK Company

1 3 5 7 9 10 8 6 4 2

Copyright © The Orion Publishing Group 2020
Map by Hemesh Alles
Illustrations by Nici Holland

By arrangement with the B B C

B B C © 1996. RADIO 4 © 2011 ARCHERS © 2010

A CIP catalogue record for this book is available from the British Library.

ISBN (Hardback) 978 1 4746 0770 4
ISBN (eBook) 978 1 4746 0771 1

Printed and bound in Great Britain by Clays Ltd, Elcograf S.p.A

MIX
Paper from
responsible sources
FSC
www.fsc.org FSC® C104740

www.weidenfeldandnicolson.co.uk
www.orionbooks.co.uk

CONTENTS

FOREWORD

Dear Reader,

You are about to embark on your village tour of Ambridge, guided by one of its most high-profile residents – Lynda Snell.

I must explain that Lynda Snell is a strange mixture of human ingredients – indeed, she has sometimes been compared to Marmite. Bossy, interfering, manipulating, devious, deeply delusional, snobbish, no self-awareness, you catch my drift. But she has a good, kind heart, compassion, energy, courage and gets things done! Her vulnerability has thrown new light on understanding her. Marmite indeed! Even after thirty-four years, I still get a kick when someone says, 'Go on, do the voice!'.

Carole Boyd (Lynda Snell)

INTRODUCTION

THE CONTROLLER OF Radio 4 said to me that when *The Archers* is on the air, all is right with the world. For nearly seventy years audiences have been able to enjoy life in Ambridge.

This last year won't be one to forget for *The Archers* – Grey Gables blew up and Lynda Snell with it, and for the first time ever we came off air – but every cloud has a silver lining. Lynda is getting better and the enforced break in transmission (we were trying to get the show back on track having binned several weeks' worth of stories because of the COVID-19 lockdown) gave us the opportunity to visit some of *The Archers* back catalogue. This has whetted our appetite, so who better to ask than Lynda Snell to use her convalescence and her matchless knowledge of Ambridge to mastermind a quiz that will test your knowledge of *The Archers* both past and present.

Lynda, now as fit as a fiddle, will take you on a tour around Ambridge – on foot, by bike and occasionally by boat drifting down the Am (but not by car – remember she is the founder member of Ambridge Speedwatch). We start at Lakey Hill, the Mount Olympus of Borsetshire, and take a sort of anticlockwise sweep around one of England's most famous villages, ending up at the Pargetter pile, Lower Loxley.

However, there is no such thing as a free lunch (even at The Bull), and on your trip Lynda will quiz you. The aim is not so much to test how hard or how long you have been listening to *The Archers*, but to dunk you in the delicious world of Ambridge trivia, and to let you discover even more about *The Archers* than you know already.

The questions come in four levels of difficulty:

- The Full Monty – simple questions that even Lynda's beloved mutt Monty would get right
- The Radio Carter – the kind of question about Ambridge gossip that if you need to phone a friend, the friend on speed dial would be Borchester Radio's 'hostess with the mostest' insider info, the one and only queen of Ambridge gossip, Susan Carter
- The Peggy Woolley – questions that will drill down into *The Archers* of yore: the kind of question that Peggy 'misses nothing remembers everything' Woolley will know the answer to
- The Jim Lloyd – the kind of fiendish question that Lynda's fellow Bull Brainbox quizzer Professor Jim Lloyd will get right

Each chapter is centred on one of the settings where the key stories of *The Archers* have taken place: Brookfield, Home Farm, The Dower House, Blossom Hill Cottage, etc. To amuse you while you are travelling from location to location, Lynda will ask you to stop a moment and reflect on all things Ambridge and ask you five sets of more wide-ranging themed questions.

Finally, chapter by chapter there is an accumulator question. Unfortunately you won't get the answer right unless you read the whole book. That, I am afraid to say, is the kind of person Lynda Snell is. Many of her fellow Ambridgeans have learnt to their cost while appearing in her famed Christmas shows that she is a harsh taskmistress, and one with strong opinions (many of which I have to say as editor I heartily disagree with): once you have started you have to finish, so there is to be no shilly-shallying once you open the book and start to explore the delights of Lynda Snell's Ambridge. The answer to this brain-teaser is hidden somewhere near the end of the book.

Beware, good luck and ENJOY!

Jeremy Howe, Editor, *The Archers*

PS: If you need help, there is a handy timeline of *The Archers* at the back of the book which may give you some clues. If you get really stuck, all of the solutions are near the back too.

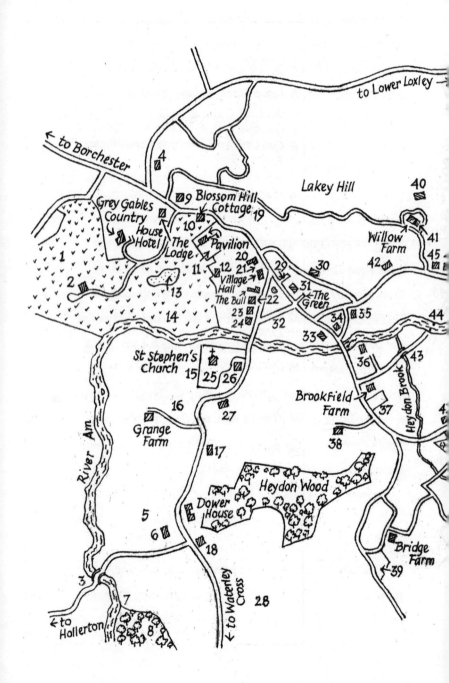

lennium
Wood
Home
Farm
idge
ll
48
Leader's
Wood
to Penny
Hassett
49
to Felpersham →
Wood

Ambridge

N
W   E
S

HEMESH. ALLES

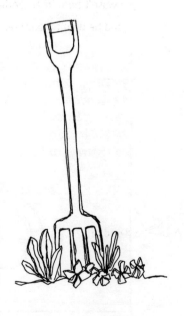

AM-GRAM

Rearrange the letters to make the name of an
Ambridge resident. There is a clue to help you.
The answer appears at the foot of the page.

RIPS DESK

He wasn't born in Ambridge
and he didn't die there.

Lakey Hill

WELCOME TO AMBRIDGE! My name is Lynda Snell, and I'm going to take you on a guided tour of the village I am proud to call my home. If you pay close attention, you may perhaps discover the answers to some of the more challenging questions in my quiz book.

We begin our tour at the top of Lakey Hill, with its magnificent view of the surrounding countryside. Behind us rise the slopes of the Hassett Hills, and over in that direction you can just make out the Lower Loxley estate, where we shall be concluding today's tour.

Looking down from this vantage point, we can see the heart of the village, The Green. Beyond it flows the River Am, and spreading out on all sides is an expanse of fields, hedgerows and woodland. As fine an example of England's green and pleasant land as you could wish to see. A pastoral idyll, that looks as if it has been there always, perfect and untouched. But a mere five years ago, that entire area was underwater. The river burst its banks, engulfing everything, including my house. And barely had we recovered from that trauma when another existential threat appeared on the horizon, in the shape of an utterly misguided plan to reroute the Borchester bypass, which would have involved driving a four-lane highway right through the heart of the village. The infamous Route B. It seems unbelievable, doesn't it, that anyone in their right mind could contemplate such desecration.

But I regret to inform you that developers, and indeed certain farmers of my acquaintance, are prone to regard our fields and meadows merely as potential building sites. Many's the battle I have fought against the despoiling of our precious countryside. Over there, in what is known as Leader's Wood, it was only my discovery of a rare and protected wild service tree that prevented the felling of that ancient woodland. Down there, in what was once Sawyer's Farm, I located an exceptional early gentian, protected under the Wildlife and Countryside Act of 1981, thus thwarting a particularly unsightly development. I'm convinced it was my discovery of rare brown hairstreak butterflies that tipped the balance, and finally saw off the egregious Route B plan.

I was less successful in my opposition to the building of *soi-disant* 'executive' housing on agricultural land over there at Bridge Farm. It broke my heart to see tons of concrete being poured into what was once not just a field, but an organic wild flower meadow. So much for Bridge Farm organics!

As I guide you around the village, I thought I might set an accumulator to sort the wheat from the chaff, as it were. Within the quiz answers, I have hidden a message for you to uncover. At each location, I will send you in search of a letter, which can be found within the answers. There are fifteen in total, and you will only find the letters by completing the quizzes. Once you have identified them, rearrange the letters and you will find a five-letter word and a ten-letter word.

When you've completed my questions about Lakey Hill, look at the answer to question 8. You need the first letter of the first word.

THE FULL MONTY

1   On a clear day, which group of hills can be seen from the top of Lakey Hill? Is it the Chilterns, the Malverns or the Mendips?

2   East of the Hill there's an Ambridge cottage that shares its name with a calendar month. What is it called? There's a one in twelve chance of being correct!

3   Lakey Hill is set in the county of Borsetshire. What is the only English county to appear as part of the first name of an Ambridge resident?

4   A lover of wild open spaces, a champion of the countryside and a thorn in the side of many farmers, which farm would Lynda do battle with if she was concerned about the fate of Lakey Hill itself?

5   At which festival is there a morning service at dawn on Lakey Hill?

THE RADIO CARTER

6 Who were the young parents of the child whose naming ceremony took place on Lakey Hill in the late nineties?

7 'Can I come home again please, Mrs Archer?' Who made this request on Lakey Hill?

8 Lakey Hill's views are unbeatable, and it's the place to enjoy the vast skies and colourful sunrises. Who toyed with the possible names Sky and Scarlett for her new baby, and what name was actually chosen?

9 Whose body was found on Lakey Hill by David and Phil while they were checking hedges?

10 Who proposed to a member of the Archer clan on Lakey Hill?

11 Shortly before their 19th birthday, one of the Archers stomped up the hill to sulk about their foiled party plans, saying, 'I don't want to be the umpteenth generation of Archers fed up on Lakey Hill.' Who was it?

THE PEGGY WOOLLEY

12 Which rather unseasonal events helped celebrate Coronation Day on Lakey Hill?

13 Lakey Hill is a favourite exercise venue for dogs and their owners. Which breed of dog was the formidable Marjorie Antrobus associated with?

14 The Lawson-Hope seat was moved from The Green and carried up to Lakey Hill by lively revellers at a house-warming party. At which cottage was the party?

15 Shula and Mark Hebden went to the top of Lakey Hill and yelled and cried to release their grief and sadness. What heartbreaking event had happened?

16 From Lakey Hill, there's a wonderful view of Ambridge and the farms around. Which farm in Ambridge has the same name as a London underground station?

17 Frank Mead would no doubt have enjoyed the golden jubilee celebrations on Lakey Hill had he still been around. He left his mark in Ambridge back in the 1960s by continually carrying out which antisocial activity?

THE JIM LLOYD

18 Which is the highest? Is it Blackpool Tower, Lakey Hill or The London Eye?

19 The colours change season by season. How many of the colours on a set of traffic lights share their names with Ambridge farms?

20 Lakey Hill produces which crop? (Don't think soil sciences or conventional arable farming.)

The Bull

THE BULL IS, as you can see, a historic half-timbered
building, and, I like to think, the epitome of the traditional
English country pub. As we move inside, you will observe
some lovely old photographs of the building, along with
a splendid collection of horse brasses. Like most country
pubs, The Bull has had to evolve with the times, with a lot
more emphasis on food rather than drink. So at the back
there is a thriving family restaurant, serving traditional
English fare, much of it locally sourced. The current chef is
a previous husband of the landlady. But he is also a master
baker: I can particularly recommend his sourdough. For the
beer drinkers amongst you, I am told that the local Shires
brewery produces a very superior pint. For those of you who
prefer something a little more sophisticated, may I suggest
our local gin, which is actually distilled here in the village.

We can take our drinks out into the beer garden,
which is presided over by a magnificent, but somewhat
aggressive, young peacock.

The Bull is currently run by Kenton Archer and his
wife, Jolene, a former country singer. I say former; she

recently attempted to revive her musical career, but one gathers it came to nothing. She was married (after divorcing the baker) to the previous landlord of The Bull, Sid Perks, having seduced him away from his then wife. It was a great scandal at the time. The pub is part-owned by another scion of the Archer clan, Lilian Bellamy, who recently took it into her head that what The Bull needed to ensure its future prosperity was a change of name. An utterly ridiculous idea. I believe she had fallen under the influence of some youthful so-called 'consultant'. So for a brief period in recent times, The Bull was known as . . . no, I simply cannot bring myself to repeat the ludicrous appellation that Lilian, and indeed Jolene and Kenton, believed would attract a younger clientele. It did of course do no such thing, and alienated a great many local and regular customers. I was personally so incensed, I chained myself to the pub sign by way of protest. Alas, to no avail. But finally, as you see, common sense prevailed and the traditional name was restored.

When you've completed my pub-related quiz, look at the answer to question 14. You need the first letter of the second word.

THE FULL MONTY

1   Jolene is a keen proponent of music nights at The
Bull, and karaoke always proves to be a popular
event. Which former Ambridge resident could have
belted out 'I'm A Tiger'?

2   Freda Fry had a pivotal role in the life of The Bull.
What was it?

3   What was The Bull rebranded as – albeit for a very
short time?

4   You would think Bull Farm House, home to local
celebrity Jean Harvey, would be in close proximity to
the hostelry which shares its name. As the crow flies,
is Bull Farm House the nearest farm to The Bull?

5   It's always easy to label people. Which person from
The Bull actually had a first name that is an anagram
of LABEL?

THE RADIO CARTER

6 Jolene Rogers changed her name in homage to a Dolly Parton country classic. What would Dolly's song have been titled had Jolene Rogers's real name been used?

7 In 2017, who proposed to whom in The Bull, although the lady in question upped and left, leaving the gentleman down on one knee?

8 The current publican Kenton eschewed all Archers to choose his best man at his wedding to Jolene. Whom did he choose instead?

9 Ted Atkins of Waterley Cross was famous for his hunting skills, which he once used at The Bull. What was his particular field of expertise?

10 A nettle-eating competition as an attraction was the brainwave of Mike Tucker. Bert Fry was the winner, but why was Nathan Booth disqualified?

11 Sid Perks once sent a Valentine's Day gift of a gold chain and heart engraved with the affectionate words 'From Sid to the love of his life'. There are several women who could have qualified for this place in Sid's heart over the years. Who was the object of his affections here?

THE PEGGY WOOLLEY

12 Prospero is a new face at The Bull. He's taken the place of one of the old regulars who met an untimely end in 2019. Who's Prospero?

13 In Coronation year, why did Peggy take on the licence for The Bull?

14 The Bull is always busy on Bonfire Night. Which owner from the pub's long and distinguished history had a first name with a link to the Gunpowder Plot?

15 Which former barmaid celebrated her nuptials the same year as Prince Charles married Lady Diana Spencer?

16 The Bull landlady Polly Perks perished in a road accident after a collision with which type of farming vehicle? Was it a combine harvester, a milk tanker or a tractor and trailer?

17 Jack Woolley and Sid Perks went back a long way. Why was it that Jack did not respond to the tragic news of Sid's sudden death?

THE JIM LLOYD

18 Does The Bull date back to the era of The Battle of Hastings between King Harold and William of Normandy, The Wars of the Roses between the Houses of York and Lancaster or the English Civil War between the Cavaliers and Roundheads?

19 What links Hollywood star Janet Leigh with would-be country star Jolene Rogers?

20 David Archer, Neil Carter and Eddie Grundy were chalking up their darts scores in The Bull one Friday night. David chalked up 28, 80 and 166 with three darts each time. Neil scored 163, 120 and 180 with three darts each time. Eddie, who was on fine form, scored 172, 180 and 180. It had been a long evening and the Shires had taken its toll. Who has made a mistake with their scoring?

The Village Green

FROM THE BULL, we move out onto the Village Green.
Take care crossing the road. Our local highways are, I
regret to say, plagued by motorists wilfully ignoring the
speed limit. So, with the help of our local police sergeant,
Harrison Burns, I have marshalled a band of local residents
into a Speedwatch unit, to photograph, shame and, one
hopes, deter such miscreants.

On your right-hand side you may observe the
Ambridge Community Shop, a thriving enterprise kept
going through the sterling efforts of a team of volunteers,
under the management of our indomitable postmistress,
Susan Carter, who not only keeps us supplied with postage
stamps, but also, for those who care to listen to it, with the
latest village gossip.

The Green is a place of communal celebration. At
Easter, there is always an egg hunt for the children, and an
Easter bonnet parade. In the past, May Day was celebrated
with dancing round the maypole, but I'm afraid in this
day and age it is well-nigh impossible to detach children
from their phones long enough for them to learn such

charming traditional customs. In summer there is the Village Fete, which has on the whole managed to maintain a traditional flavour, with a tombola, a white elephant stall and the Edgeley Morris Men. There have been attempts at innovation over the years, some more successful than others. Spile troshing, I seem to recall – don't ask me to explain. Ferret racing. Dunk the vicar. Now that has proved perennially popular, and is endured, I have to say, with commendable good humour by our present incumbent, Alan Franks. I stepped into the breach myself last year, when Alan was unfortunately unavailable. Not something I have any desire to repeat. But, as with The Bull, more recent attempts to drag the Fete into the twenty-first century by pandering to the tastes of today's young people have not ended well. A bid to replace the splendid Hollerton Silver Band with a so-called 'grunge' band happily came to nothing, when members of that particular ensemble fell out over, so I am told, artistic differences.

On 5 November we meet up again to celebrate Guy Fawkes Night, which always features, as well as a splendid firework display, a mighty bonfire. I have on occasion had to insist on the bonfire being rebuilt at the last minute, because hedgehogs make a habit of sheltering in such structures, and I simply cannot countenance the possibility of 'hogicide'.

Then in early December, there is the switching on of the Christmas lights. Tradition has it that the houses around The Green turn on their lights in a particular order. And with the accompaniment of roast chestnuts and mulled wine, it is a delightful prelude to the Christmas season.

Once you've puzzled your way around The Green, look at the answer to question 20. You need the first letter of the first word.

THE FULL MONTY

1   Ambridge's Village Green is which geometrical shape? Is it circular, rectangular or triangular?

2   Which traditionally comes first in the Ambridge year, the Village Fete or the Flower and Produce Show?

3   Brother and sister Tom and Helen Archer have both lived at separate times in a flat above what?

4   What is the link between the church in Ambridge and the day after Christmas?

5   Which word completed Walter Gabriel's customary greeting, 'Hello me old pal, me old _____!'?

THE RADIO CARTER

6 An unwelcome face from the past linked to historical child abuse caused Village Green resident Jim Lloyd to make a dramatic exit from the Tearoom. The event should have been a happy one. What event was it?

7 George and Christine Barford, who lived at the police house, were awarded first place in the National Garden Scheme Open Gardens in May 2003. Which celebrity gardener judged the Ambridge entries?

8 Whose house move involved three very different residences: The Stables, Lower Loxley and No. 1 The Green?

9 Never one to miss the merest whiff of scandal, Susan became suspicious in the village shop when Lexi bought what, alerting the ever-watchful Mrs Carter to the fact that Lexi might be pregnant? Was it alcohol-free beer, decaffeinated coffee or fruit juice?

10 In a wartime-themed Village Fete, David, Kenton and Nigel appeared as which unlikely trio?

11 Tongues were wagging when Polly Perks took on the village shop. How did she find the funds to do this?

THE PEGGY WOOLLEY

12 You would think that the police house on The Green would be a safe place to be. What was the eventual fate of this building after it became a domestic residence?

13 Glebelands, on the south side of The Green, was a development of executive houses built in the late 1970s. Which individual was the driving force behind it: Jack Woolley, Nigel Pargetter or Matt Crawford?

14 When expressing mild surprise, Jethro Larkin, a long-standing resident of The Green, referred to which part of his anatomy?

15 In the 1950s why was the number 14 an important number for the village shop?

16 What is the link between the *Angel of the North* and the Village Fete?

17 Martha Woodford took it upon herself to keep clean and decorate with hanging flower baskets which Ambridge landmark?

THE JIM LLOYD

18 The Great Grange Farm car boot sale of 1996 was held to raise much-needed funds for which village amenity?

19 You are celebrating your birthday with a fete in early May on the Village Green. With which building do you have a natural affinity?

20 If a certain village cottage was known by its scientific name it would be marked on the map as Lonicera Cottage. How is it better known to the people of Ambridge?

Reflections:
Out of Ambridge

AS WE CROSS the River Am, and stroll down towards the church, let me challenge you with some oblique brain-teasers, not specifically tied to village locations. While it's hard to see why anyone would ever wish to venture far from this place, life does go on in the rest of the world. So these are questions involving events beyond the boundaries of Ambridge.

1 Jill's dapper love interest harks from outside of Ambridge. Where did Jill Archer and Leonard Berry first meet?

2 The railway line passing west of Ambridge has a rather fruity name. What is the line called – the Apple Line, the Blackberry Line or the Orange Line?

3 Tom's wife and mother are not locals. Both hail from which part of the UK?

4 Which pub landlord died unexpectedly while visiting his daughter Lucy in New Zealand?

5 There isn't a railway station in Ambridge, but what is the name of the nearest station to Ambridge?

6   Which Ambridge resident was born at a mud-soaked Glastonbury Festival when Blur, Bob Dylan and Tony Bennett were all headline acts?

7   This pair moved to Ambridge in 2013, but their relationship didn't last long and both ultimately left the village: one to Hampshire, the other to Minneapolis. Which couple was this?

8   Which couple headed for Nashville, Tennessee, spiritual home of country music, to celebrate their honeymoon? Was it Eddie and Clarrie, Roy and Hayley or Sid and Jolene?

9   Which market town in West Yorkshire combines the surname of an Ambridge family and the name of an Ambridge farm?

10   In what particular location did Cameron Fraser abandon Elizabeth, when she believed they were going away on holiday together?

11 What is the number of the A road between Ambridge and Borchester? It's the same number as the year Bill Clinton was elected US president and the Summer Olympics were held in Barcelona.

12 Whose children have Xhosa first names and reside in South Africa? What are the children called?

13 In which far from romantic setting did the Reverend Alan Franks propose to Usha Gupta?

14 In the mid-1980s, Elizabeth came third in the Penny Hassett pancake race. The fact that she, and not the winner, had her photo in the *Felpersham Evening Post* may well have had something to do with her outfit. What was she dressed as?

15 The Old Corn Mill has been revamped into a fashionable hostelry, enjoying a riverside location in Borchester. It went by a different name when Eddie Grundy had his first legal pint in a pub there. What was it known as then? Was it The Dirty Duck, The Goat and Nightgown or The Pig and Ferret?

16 When Tom Archer jilted Kirsty he left for Canada, while Kirsty went to their intended honeymoon destination. Where did she go and with whom?

17 What sounds like there should be a connection between the poignant First World War song 'Roses of Picardy' and an area south of Ambridge?

18 The Tregorrans had close ties with Ambridge over many years, and stayed in touch with residents even after they moved to Bristol. They made at least two visits in the first decade of the millennium, one for a very happy occasion and one for a sad one. What were these occasions?

19 During the struggle to find a solution to the inheritance at Brookfield, David and Ruth considered moving away to where? Was it Australia, France or the USA?

20 For the first few years of his life, Brian's son Ruairi spoke chiefly which language?

St Stephen's Church

AS WE PASS through the lychgate into the churchyard, you
will observe, in the shade of the ancient yew trees, a very
recent grave. That is the resting place of Joe Grundy, who
died recently at the age of ninety-eight. In his younger
days he was something of a reprobate, a poacher and
petty criminal. But he was the last of a generation of true
countrymen, becoming in old age something of a local
treasure, trotting round the lanes in his pony and trap,
growing prize-winning vegetables, or occupying his corner
in The Bull, consuming pints of cider, usually bought
by other people. He was a fount of knowledge about
the history, myths and ghosts of Borsetshire, though the
provenance of some of his tales did not, it has to be said,
bear close examination.

This church, St Stephen's, is known to have been built
on the site of an early seventh-century Augustinian church,
and recent excavations suggest an even earlier origin.

In recent years, to the particular delight of my husband,
Robert, a keen ornithologist, we have had a peregrine
falcon nesting on the church roof. A rather less welcome

form of wildlife arrived some years ago, in the form of an infestation of mice, which ate through the leather organ stops. Considerable fundraising was required to make good the damage. That is a disadvantage of having such a venerable edifice in the village; there is always some element of the structure in need of restoration. Almost every other year, it seems to me, the proceeds of the Village Fete have gone into repairs to the church roof. Or so the vicar tells us.

However the most recent project in aid of the church has nothing to do with fundraising. Shula Hebden Lloyd, a devout woman who is currently training for the priesthood, proposed, in her wisdom, that a work of art should be created that would inspire quiet contemplation. However, the committee that assembled – of which I was regrettably a member – to consider the various proposals disagreed so profoundly that discussion frequently descended into a shouting match. And the announcement of the winner, which I understand Shula selected by sticking a pin in the list of submissions, has only served to provoke more discord. So much for quiet contemplation.

However there is already much great artistry inside the church: the fine stonework, the stained-glass windows, and indeed some exquisite tapestry hassocks, made by the WI (of which I am a member) and residents of the Laurels to replace the kneelers which were shockingly stolen some years ago.

Before you move on from these hallowed grounds, look at the answer to question 9. You need the first letter of the third word.

THE FULL MONTY

1 Where is the nearest cathedral city to Ambridge?

2 Who would have a sound reason for visiting St Stephen's? Would it be a campanologist, a numismatist or a philatelist? (Don't try saying this after a few pints of Shires!)

3 Which Ambridge resident shares her first name with a book of the Old Testament?

4 Valda replaced which church stalwart at St Stephen's, and in what capacity?

5 On Kirsty and Tom's big day, where did Tom break the news that the wedding was off? Was it at the altar, at the church door or in the vestry?

THE RADIO CARTER

6 Which spouse of a convicted criminal has been a churchwarden at St Stephen's?

7 What in particular did Peggy Woolley disapprove of regarding Alan Franks' predecessor at St Stephen's?

8 Which aristocratic friend of Caroline's took Mark and Shula's wedding photos?

9 When Lynda took part in the Ambridge Three Peaks Challenge, she and her costume got stuck in the church tower. What was she dressed as? Was it a church bell, a Fabergé egg or a piebald llama?

10 Shula and Richard Locke were once romantically involved. They met up again some years later at St Stephen's after which musical event?

11 Architecturally, is St Stephen's vicarage a Georgian former gentleman's residence, a thatched cottage or a 1970s bungalow?

THE PEGGY WOOLLEY

12 At whose funeral was Oasis's 'Wonderwall' played as a tribute?

13 In 1959 a stained-glass window in St Stephen's was dedicated to the memory of which member of the Archer family?

14 What farming-linked costume was Usha Gupta wearing when she was given a lift by vicar Alan Franks on his motorbike after the Felpersham charity run?

15 What was being installed in the church when carbon dating proved that the foundations of an earlier building dated back to the sixth century AD?

16 Now buried at St Stephen's, in which property nearby did long-term Brookfield owner Phil Archer finally pass away, and which piece of music was playing when he was discovered by his wife, Jill? Was it J.S. Bach's 'Sheep May Safely Graze', Beethoven's *Pastoral Symphony* or Sir Edward Elgar's *The Dream of Gerontius*?

17 Zebedee Tring, who is buried at St Stephen's, shared his first name with a character from the iconic TV series *The Magic Roundabout*. Which other long-term Ambridge resident can say the same?

THE JIM LLOYD

18 In the 1990s Tom Forrest placed a stuffed owl behind the pulpit. This was no act of pagan worship but an interesting, if bizarre, experiment to try and scare something away. What was Tom trying to scare?

19 Which vicar would have been particularly helpful with looking after Baby Spice, Posh Spice and Ginger Spice?

20 Robin Stokes had a stag night in the 1990s on a day with special religious significance. The evening involved taking part in a competitive event. What was that day and the event?

AM-GRAM

Rearrange the letters to make the name of an
Ambridge resident. There is a clue to help you.
The answer appears at the foot of the page.

PREACH ART

This would have to be done
organically of course.

Grange Farm

I HAVE ALREADY mentioned the late Joe Grundy, who rented this farm from what was originally the Lawson-Hope, later Bellamy, estate. The tenancy was passed on to his son, Eddie, who, like his father, was something of a ne'er-do-well, until he had the good sense to marry Clarrie Larkin. When Robert and I first came to Ambridge in the 1980s, this fine house was a sorry sight: slates missing from the roof, window frames rotting and the surrounding yard filled with ancient, rusting bits of machinery. But somehow Joe and Eddie contrived to make a living, until the turn of the millennium, when they could no longer pay the rent and were summarily evicted. The house was then sold, and, along with fifty acres of land, was acquired by Oliver Sterling who had the building stripped out and thoroughly restored, and lived here with his wife, Caroline, until her untimely death in 2017.

But by an extraordinary twist of fate, or rather a supremely selfless act of generosity by Oliver Sterling, the Grundy family are now back living in the farmhouse which, as you may observe, is gradually reverting to its former state of decrepitude. The garden is overrun with pigs, the yard has acquired several bits of rusting machinery, and over there is a large, shabby-looking caravan, home to young Ed Grundy and his family, parked, I am sure, in breach of local government regulations. If I were in Oliver Sterling's shoes, I should have a thing or two to say about that. And according to Susan Carter, the interior of the house is faring no better, because of Joe's, and now Eddie's, complete inability to keep their pet ferrets from venturing indoors and wreaking havoc on the soft furnishings.

In another act of extreme generosity Oliver has given the Grange Farm orchard over to the community. However, it is still the Grundys who largely reap the benefit, being, as they are, traditional cider makers. Not a beverage that appeals to me, I have to say. But there is an enthusiastic fraternity of aficionados, known as the Cider Club. I say fraternity, as it is largely a male affair. But Lilian Bellamy is apparently a member. Well, drinking has always been one of her favourite pastimes.

Once you have attempted all the questions about this chaotic farm, look at the answer to question 7. You need the first letter of the second word.

THE FULL MONTY

1   William and Emma Grundy's first child was named after an Ambridge resident who had shown great kindness to young Will. Who was this?

2   Joe Grundy spent his final evening at Grange Farm, engaged in one of his favourite activities. Was it cider drinking or ferret racing?

3   Eddie's mate Paul shares a descriptive name with a larger than life *Thomas the Tank Engine* character. What is it?

4   What is the name of the mobile home Emma set up at Grange Farm where she welcomed Ed back into the family?

5   On the evening of her first hen night Emma slept with her future husband's brother, Ed. What did she do on her second hen night more than a decade later?

THE RADIO CARTER

6 Which two places did the Grundys call home after their eviction from Grange Farm and before settling at Keeper's Cottage?

7 Joe Grundy nicknamed which Ambridge resident the 'dog woman'? Was it Marjorie Antrobus, Lynda Snell or Carol Tregorran?

8 Why could the audience have doubled up with laughter watching Eddie Grundy's performances as Wishee Washee in *Aladdin*?

9 In which receptacle were the apples pasteurised for the Grange Farm Cider Club?

10 What chronic complaint did Joe Grundy suffer from, usually when there was work to be done? Was it farmer's lung, pigman's knee or reaper's hip?

11 As he neared his hundredth birthday, Joe Grundy looked forward to receiving a telegram from HM the Queen. The nearest thing to this arrived during his wake. What was it?

THE PEGGY WOOLLEY

12 When Prince Charles and Lady Diana Spencer's engagement was announced, what was Clarrie Larkin heard singing? Was it 'Congratulations', 'I'm Getting Married in the Morning' or 'Some Day My Prince Will Come'?

13 Aged twelve and out trick-or-treating for Halloween, what unusual headgear did William Grundy wear?

14 Which Grundy proposed to Emma Carter first? (It wasn't Joe.)

15 Back in his country singing days, Eddie released a single when a vinyl record had an A side and a B side. Side A's title featured the name of farm animals and side B name checked his wife. What were the two titles?

16 Who confided to Ed Grundy, 'I've got hidden shallows, me!'?

17 After their eviction from Grange Farm, who had the unenviable task of locking the back door for the very last time?

THE JIM LLOYD

18 Which Grundy's first name can be made from the letters on the top row of a QWERTY typewriter?

19 If Bert Fry's status was gold and Jim Lloyd's status was platinum, what would it apply to?

20 Which two words complete the verse on a sampler made by Susan Grundy, Eddie's late mother?

'Laughter is like music
That lingers in the heart,
And when its melody is heard
The ills of _ _ _ _ _ _ _ _ _ _'

The Dower House

WHAT CAN ONE say about the Dower House? It is a substantial and extremely desirable residence, with splendid views and an extensive garden. It is now the property of one Justin Elliott, a relative newcomer to the village, who is, I regret to say, a property developer. As such, he has no conscience, riding roughshod over the history and traditions of Ambridge when there is money to be made. He was responsible for the Beechwood estate, not to mention the transformation of Berrow Farm into an indoor penitentiary for dairy cows. When that failed to make a profit, he turned it instead into a giant pig factory. And his partner in crime is Lilian Bellamy, as I have previously mentioned, part-owner of The Bull. Which is where, incidentally, she grew up; her father was the pub landlord. But she subsequently married Ralph Bellamy, heir to the Bellamy estate, which in those days owned half of Ambridge.

They went to live on Guernsey, where Lilian remained after Ralph's death, only reappearing some twenty years ago with a toy boy called Scott. A former Butlin's Redcoat, as I recall, with a penchant for motorbikes. And when he, predictably, left her for someone his own age, she fell in with self-styled 'entrepreneur' Matt Crawford, whom everyone bar Lilian could see was a con man, and ended up in prison. What Lilian ever saw in him is a complete mystery. And what Justin sees in her . . . he could have found someone a great deal younger, and without such a dubious past. He's a very wealthy businessman and remarkably well preserved, although for all I know he could share Lilian's penchant for hair dye and plastic surgery.

This house also boasts a stable block. But as far as I know it's standing empty. Lilian is an enthusiastic horsewoman and Justin owns two fine Arab horses, but they are kept in livery at the Ambridge Stables. I suppose she regards grooming and mucking out as beneath her these days.

I have to confess that Lilian and I are distantly related, in that her son James is the partner of my stepdaughter Leonie. So we are both grandmothers to their son, Mungo. Devoted as I am to little Mungo, I make sure that Lilian and I rub along together.

While we're here, let's continue with the accumulator. Look at the answer to question 19. You need the first letter of the first word.

THE FULL MONTY

1   Which of Toby Fairbrother's business interests would have a particular appeal to Lilian?

2   What type of building, crucial to livestock farmers, did Justin Elliott want to turn into offices?

3   Lilian was less than thrilled to receive a Ruby from Matt Crawford, but this was no gemstone. What's Ruby?

4   The Dower House has been home, at different times, to which two formidable females who have both had a financial interest in The Bull?

5   In order to boost her morale, what cosmetic procedure did Lilian have, when Matt abandoned her?

THE RADIO CARTER

6 Lilian was persuaded to buy an exclusive cosmetic called Lipoflora. Why should she have been suspicious when her search proved fruitless?

7 'A balding, middle-aged man who overestimates his attractiveness to younger women.' Yes, it could apply to virtually anyone, but to whom was Lilian actually referring?

8 Eddie once interrupted milkman Mike Tucker and Lilian (in her dressing gown). What was going on? Was Lilian teaching Mike how to mix cocktails, was Mike passing on his ballroom dancing skills, or was it something else entirely?

9 When Justin and Lilian's affair was still a secret, and they were sharing an illicit bottle of Dom Pérignon, a chance visit by Justin's wife Miranda caused Lilian to flee dressed in a negligee, fur coat and what?

10 Who said this, and to whom? 'I couldn't let the loveliest woman I ever met go, without her knowing how I felt.'

11 When Eddie carried a box of Borchester slipware into the Dower House for Lilian, what did he mistakenly think it contained?

THE PEGGY WOOLLEY

12 In which rather unusual way did Lilian's first husband meet his demise, and in what type of building did this take place?

13 Which owner of the Dower House was responsible for Elizabeth Archer seeking an abortion?

14 Matt wasn't always the most popular of people. Who trained his dog to growl every time the name Crawford was mentioned?

15 The rooms at the Dower House which Matt Crawford used as an office were originally used by which member of the household?

16 Matt was hoping Lilian would be a sleeping partner in his property business as well as his private life, but that isn't Lilian's style. What was the name of the company they both owned and both took an active part in?

17 Which Dower House housekeeper shared her surname with the name of another Ambridge property? Was it Mrs Blossom, Mrs Greenwood or Mrs Woodbine?

THE JIM LLOYD

18 Who married and took up residence in the Dower House the year England defended their football World Cup crown?

19 What links Lilian's honeymoon after her second marriage and a Gilbert and Sullivan opera?

20 Each letter in the names of these Ambridge residents has been replaced by a number. Each number is different. The total value of each name is found by adding individual numbers together. If ALAN = 8, and IAN = 6, what is LILIAN worth?

Reflections:
All Creatures
Great and Small

BEFORE WE TAKE to the water, let us relax a while here by the river, and I shall set you another modest challenge, this time concerning the animal kingdom. Feathered, furry and four-legged friends are integral to Ambridge life, both as pets, pests and produce. This is their moment to shine.

1   Which sophisticated beverage is surprisingly named after a German shepherd cross rescue dog?

2   Wolfgang and Constanza made their mark as Ambridge residents. Who or what were they?

3   Sisters-in-law Pat and Jennifer share what some might say is an agricultural star sign. What is it?

4   When Joe adopted Basil, the talking parrot, what did young William try to teach the bird to do?

5   Kirsty told Tom she was going to become a mother after which pantomime?

6   What colour connected the names of Christine Archer's horse Link and Lilian Archer's horse Knight?

7   To the good people of Ambridge, who were Persephone and Demeter? Were they two of Jazzer's favourite pigs, goats owned by Lynda Snell or Justin Elliott's horses?

8   What did Jethro Larkin's dog Gyp share with his master each evening before he had his dinner? Was it a cup of tea, a sip of Shires or a walk round the garden?

9   Who had the inscription 'Well done, thou good and faithful servant' on their headstone?

10   LUSCINIA MEGARHYNCHOS is a bit of a mouthful for a farm name, yet that is how it may be referred to in scientific circles. What is the everyday name of this farm?

11 Eddie named a pig after a glamorous sci-fi character. Was it Barbarella, Princess Leia or Superwoman?

12 What is a Borsetshire Beauty and why might it have painful associations for the Fairbrothers?

13 Which of Eddie's ferrets shared its name with a Shakespearean character?

14 When the Fairbrother boys arrived in Ambridge in 2015, which Christmas fare did they plan to produce and why did it rile the Grundys?

15 Clarrie and Eddie replaced Mike and Eddie. Then Robert and Lynda replaced Clarrie and Eddie. What were they doing?

16 In what capacity was Basil replaced by Benjamin?

17 Which animals were an unwelcome welcoming committee for the Snells on their first day in Ambridge?

18 Over the years this land has housed sheep, calves and even a pair of barn owls. Originally a farm in its own right, Marneys became part of which farm's estate?

19 In 1999, Eddie managed to trick Joe into taking photographs of the animals on the farm. It was an April Fool, but what did Eddie tell Joe the photos would be used for?

20 A tank kept in Jim's living room always proves to be a talking point for visitors. Does it contain tropical fish, a corn snake or a tarantula?

The Am

WE WILL NOW take to the water and row gently down-stream. When Robert and I first moved to Ambridge, we were thrilled to have the waters of the River Am lapping at the bottom of our garden. The water was clear and clean, popular with anglers, and indeed wild swimmers. Robert spent many a happy hour on the lookout for kingfishers. But some sixteen years later, we felt rather differently, when torrential rain caused the river level to rise to such an extent that it flooded our garden, and, worse still, parts of the house. We were assured that this was a once-in-a-lifetime event. But of course in 2015, there was the catastrophic flood which overwhelmed not just riverside properties like ours, but the entire village.

It did cross our mind that it would be wise to move to a higher location. But with so many of our neighbours in the same boat, so to speak, we decided that a bit of solidarity was called for. In any case, it would have been impossible to sell the house.

But disaster struck again in 2017, when the clear waters of the Am became mysteriously polluted with some noxious substance. The contamination was traced back to Low Mead, a particular area of Home Farm where there appeared to have been some toxic waste illegally dumped back in the 1970s. Brian Aldridge, the owner of Home Farm, categorically denied any involvement in this, but it was subsequently proved that he was being economical with the truth, and had personally sanctioned the use of Low Mead as a dump. He was therefore liable for the cost of the clean-up operation, which, since there was also contamination of the groundwater, was astronomical.

The consequences for the Aldridges were devastating. Brian's reputation as an upstanding member of the community was considerably tarnished. Not before time, in my opinion. He has always exhibited that sense of entitlement, commonplace amongst the land-owning classes, which precludes them from considering what effect their actions might have on their tenants, neighbours or indeed their family. In this case, it was Brian's wife, Jennifer, a completely innocent party, who suffered the most, and had to make the greatest sacrifice.

If you are keeping a written record of the accumulator, hold on to it tightly as you don't want the waters of the Am to wash away your hard work. Look at the answer to question 19. You need the first letter of the first word.

THE FULL MONTY

1 Who had to sell the family home after dead fish started to appear in the Am in 2017?

2 Is St Stephen's Church north or south of the River Am? Flip a coin if you are uncertain!

3 Close to Millennium Wood, a very narrow bridge crosses the Am. Why might villagers be reluctant to cross it?

4 The Am is a more famous waterway, but which river in Borsetshire shares its name with a fish?

5 In Ambridge, how many roads in the form of bridges cross the Am? Is there one, four or ten?

THE RADIO CARTER

6 Because of a disaster with the Am in 2015, what was the upstairs function room at The Bull renamed?

7 What event was taking place at The Bull when the Am flooded in 2015? Was it a curry night, a fancy dress evening or a karaoke night?

8 Which keen wild swimmer's dip in the Am in January 2018 led to an investigation into the serious pollution of the river?

9 The poor Am has had its waters sullied on a number of occasions. In 1989 Phil Archer was found guilty of polluting the Am. What was the pollutant: animal carcasses, an old tractor or slurry?

10 In 2017, suspicions around pollution arose when which creature protected by the Wildlife & Countryside Act 1981 was found dead in the Am?

11 In response to a challenge to swim naked in the Am, who said, 'Do I really want to show my naked bottom to Jazzer McCreary?'?

THE PEGGY WOOLLEY

12 Who rescued Freda Fry when she was trapped in her car as the flood waters rose in 2015?

13 Which late resident of Ambridge has a bridge over Heydon Brook, which flows into the Am, named in his honour?

14 Which of the following landmarks do not back on to the Am – The Bull, Bluebell Cottage or Nightingale Farm?

15 Whose new year got off to a bad start when he was crushed by a frightened cow, which had managed to slip down a bank into a ravine?

16 Lynda and Robert Snell were flooded out of Ambridge Hall by an overpowering Am in which jubilee year of HM the Queen? Was it her silver, golden or diamond jubilee?

17 Rob Titchener was the hero of the hour during the floods of March 2015 when he saved Shula, Alistair and Christine when which building flooded?

THE JIM LLOYD

18 Which item of clothing is needed to complete the original name of the Am?

19 What links a Schubert quintet, a ship in the classic radio series *The Navy Lark* and creatures reintroduced to the Am after pollution?

20 What started at The Bull, paused briefly by the pond, went to the churchyard, stopped off at a bridge over the Am, moved on to Ambridge Hall and then on to the Millennium Wood?

Brookfield

THERE HAVE BEEN Archers at Brookfield farm for as long as anyone can remember, firstly as tenants of the Lawson-Hope estate, and then as owners, when in 1954 the present incumbent David Archer's grandfather bought it from the Lawson-Hopes. The house is brick and timber, dating from the sixteenth century, and across the yard is the bijou Rickyard Cottage. There is another dwelling, a bungalow, built for David and his wife, Ruth, when they were first married, and now occupied by Bert Fry, a former employee of the farm. Being on the riverbank, it was, like my house, inundated by the flood, which led to the tragic death of Bert's wife, Freda.

Brookfield is essentially a dairy farm, admirable in that their cows graze outside for most of the year, unlike so many modern dairy farms, which keep the poor creatures the entire time in sheds. They also run a herd of Hereford cattle, providing top-quality 'grass-fed' beef. But since these days we are all being exhorted to eat less meat and dairy, one can but wonder how sustainable a model this is.

The most interesting building on the farm is an
ancient barn, of the same vintage, I should imagine,
as the farmhouse. It came to my notice when I was
planning a production, not of a play by Shakespeare
(though my *A Midsummer Night's Dream* is still spoken
of in the village), but of *The Canterbury Tales*. For more
years than I care to remember, I have been producer,
director and frequently dramaturg of Christmas
pantomimes and other theatrical events in Ambridge.
The Canterbury Tales was to be my swansong, and I had a
vision of the villagers assembling by the light of flaming
torches, and like the pilgrims of old, seating themselves
on straw bales in this ancient barn, to be entertained. I
did not predict the battle that followed with the Health
and Safety Department of Borsetshire Council. But
artistic endeavour triumphed over bureaucracy, and
the production was, though I say it myself, a stunning
success. Ruth Archer played Chaucer, which took some
persuasion; she has never been a willing participant in
village entertainment. But I felt that her Northumbrian
accent, undimmed even after thirty-odd years' residence
in Borsetshire, echoes the kind of resonance one finds
in Chaucer's Middle English. '*Whan that Aprill, with
his shoures soote, The droghte of March hath perced to the
roote . . .*' Beautiful.

Such was the renown of my production that that barn became something of a local attraction, and David realised what a treasure he possessed, and had spent his life failing to notice.

Speaking of treasure, how are you getting on with hunting down the answers to the accumulator? Look at the answer to question 11. You need the first letter of the first word.

THE FULL MONTY

1   A conscientious, hard-working farmer all his working life, Dan Archer died of a heart attack trying to rescue an animal which had rolled onto its back. Was it a cow, a pig or a sheep?

2   Who was David and Ruth's eldest child named after?

3   Whose engagement party, set to be held at the Brookfield barn, was cancelled due to the 2020 lockdown?

4   Whose childhood nickname was Snowball, and why?

5   Who bought Ben his first car, which received howls of derision because of its garish colour? Was it David and Ruth, Jill and Leonard or Kenton and Jolene?

THE RADIO CARTER

6 Lynda's masterpiece of a production of *The Canterbury Tales* was universally hailed as a triumph. When a vital prop went missing, however, the production was in jeopardy. What was this vital prop, and what was its replacement made from?

7 The enigmatic Nelson Gabriel sold which business to Kenton Archer?

8 What did Elizabeth Archer throw at Robin Fairbrother when he broke up with her?

9 Ruth's mother, Heather Pritchard, and Jill Archer crossed swords over which breakfast item?

10 David cooked supper for the children when Ruth was visiting 'an old friend'. The friend in question was cowman Sam Batton, but at the eleventh hour Ruth did not go through with their affair. More importantly, what was David cooking for the children?

11 Among the Archer siblings, who initially disputed Phil's plans for the inheritance of the family estate? Was it Elizabeth, David, Kenton or Shula?

THE PEGGY WOOLLEY

12 Everyone experienced lockdown in 2020, but Brookfield experienced this in 2001. Why?

13 At which farm was Ruth a lodger while she was doing work experience as a student at Brookfield?

14 Which romantic event were David Archer and Sophie Barlow watching on TV when he proposed marriage?

15 Why would the classic English nursery rhyme 'Three Blind Mice' bring back chilling memories for Elizabeth?

16 Inside Brookfield, David, Ruth and family sat down to watch a *Transformers* film in July 2012. What ended up being transformed outside?

17 Whose name from a Beatles song title would bring back unhappy memories for Pip?

THE JIM LLOYD

18 Which member of the Archer clan has a first name where all the letters read in alphabetical order?

19 Brookfield is at the centre of four medieval fields in Ambridge. Brook Field and Lakey Hill Field are two of them. The other two are named after compass points. What are they called, and what are the odds on you getting the answer correct?

20 The middle names of Kenton and David combine to make the name of a poet, who wrote about his love of nature and the countryside, and was much admired by John Tregorran. Who was the poet?

AM-GRAM

Rearrange the letters to make the name of an Ambridge resident. There is a clue to help you. The answer appears at the foot of the page.

JOLLY DIM

This resident certainly professes not to be!

Bridge Farm

AND SO WE come to Bridge Farm, and another branch of
the Archer clan. Unlike his sister Lilian, Tony Archer has
never strayed beyond the bounds of Ambridge, and it is
said of him that he has never knowingly been caught being
cheerful. Mind you, he and his wife, Pat have had a lot to
contend with over the years. Their elder son died in an
accident twenty-odd years ago, their daughter Helen was
sent to prison for attacking her abusive and controlling
husband, and as for younger son, Tom . . . I suppose one
could be charitable and say he has been struggling all this
time to fill the boots of his dead brother. For years he kept
pigs, and had some success with his sausage enterprise.
But recently, since his marriage to Natasha Thomas, he's
given up on pig-keeping. And talking of marriage, Tom
has made rather a pig's ear of things in that department.
He was all set to marry his previous girlfriend, Kirsty
Miller, but notoriously jilted her on the wedding day. It
was a great scandal at the time, and Tom effectively had
to flee the country, moving to Canada for several months.
He married Natasha in such haste, after the briefest of

courtships. Not many people know this, but she walked out on him very shortly after the marriage. They seem to have made up now, but I wouldn't put money on that relationship lasting the course. In my opinion, the most promising member of the Bridge Farm family is Johnny Phillips, offspring of dead son John, whose existence only came to light in recent years, but who has proved to be a true son of the soil, a conscientious farmer and an honest and straightforward young man.

Bridge Farm's main claim to fame is that it has been organic since 1984. The success of that venture is, I believe, almost wholly due to the dairy enterprise of Tony's wife, Pat, whose yoghurt and ice cream are sold throughout Borsetshire. But as I have previously mentioned, the family's principles did not inhibit their sale of three and a half acres of beautiful organic meadow to Justin Elliott. The result? A blot on the Ambridge landscape. I was asked by the publisher to have a whole chapter about Beechwood, but as far as I'm concerned it does not exist. So I refused.

You're over halfway through the accumulator now. Look at the answer to question 19. You need the first letter of the first word.

THE FULL MONTY

1   Who took over the tenancy of Bridge Farm in the year of the Queen's silver jubilee?

2   Much to Lynda Snell's horror, the Archers sold a parcel of Bridge Farm land to Justin Elliott for the creation of a property development, which became the Beechwood housing estate. Pat and Tony were not usually considered to be an affluent branch of the Archer clan; nevertheless these three and a half acres of land were sold for a goodly sum. Was it £500,000, £1 million or £3 million?

3   It sounds like it ought to be, but is Bridge Farm situated near a bridge? You have a 50:50 chance with this!

4   Where on the farm did Tony Archer suffer a heart attack?

5   Which former Bridge Farm worker used their severance pay to buy a tarantula?

THE RADIO CARTER

6   Who moved the congregation with his reading of a poem at John Archer's funeral, and surprised everyone later when they found out he had also written it?

7   Some French visitors arrived at Bridge Farm in 2019. Were they exchange students, Soil Association inspectors or dairy cattle?

8   Tony Archer was critically injured by Otto. Who or what was Otto – a Borchester nightclub bouncer, a prize bull or a casual crop picker?

9   Which two personal disasters led to a near fatal eating disorder for Helen Archer?

10   Pat Lewis proposed to Tony Archer. Was it a leap year?

11   Which accommodation was provided for single mum Sharon Richards at Bridge Farm? Was it a holiday let, a caravan or a spare bedroom?

THE PEGGY WOOLLEY

12 Who started delivery of Bridge Farm's veg boxes and why was it convenient for him?

13 At the start of the new millennium, what was the name of the shop opened by Pat and Tony in Borchester?

14 In 2002, Tony was gifted some money by Peggy, which he used to buy a car. What was his sporty vehicle of choice?

15 When Pat Archer cancelled her husband's *Daily Express* without telling him, which daily newspaper did she order in its place?

16 What life-changing event did John Archer discuss the night before he died?

17 Helen Archer developed a product called Sterling Gold with the support of Oliver Sterling. Was this a dry cider, a cheese or a blend of coffee?

THE JIM LLOYD

18 In which year, a year shared by the title of an iconic book, did Pat and Tony become organic farmers?

19 In an early 1980s fundraiser for Borchester General Hospital, the great and good of Ambridge went to a fancy dress ball at the County Hotel. Nigel Pargetter was dressed as a gorilla of course. Brian Aldridge went as the Scarlet Pimpernel. With possible delusions of grandeur, what character did Tony Archer go as?

20 Why could the nickname of long-serving Manchester United manager Alex Ferguson (Fergie) cause so much heartache to Pat and Tony Archer?

Reflections:
What's Your
Emergency?

IT WILL TAKE a while to walk to our next destination, so let us keep those brains ticking over with some reflections on the less tranquil side of village life. Ambridge may seem like a pastoral idyll, but many are the villagers who have found themselves on the wrong side of the law, and like the rest of us, they have had to face up to accident, illness and indeed death. *Et in Arcadia Ego*, as Jim Lloyd would probably say.

1   Never one to back off from an attention-grabbing headline, what was the *Borchester Echo* headline referring to when it read 'Rural Idyll Rocked by Brutal Attack'?

2   At a protest in Borchester which missile did Jill Archer throw at the unfortunate Lulu Duxford? Was it an egg, a flapjack or an ice cream?

3   Rex Fairbrother's rugby career was cut short due to an injury. What did he injure?

4   Nic Grundy died suddenly after contracting sepsis. What did she confess to on her deathbed?

5   Over time, Harrison Burns has arrested Jill Archer, Freddie Pargetter and Wayne Tucson. Starting with the first, can you say in which order he arrested them?

6   What was the charge when Susan Carter was given a six-month prison sentence in the early 1990s?

7   Which father and son both broke collarbones in riding accidents?

8   Back in the 1950s, on what special occasion was Tom Forrest overwhelmed to hear the music of the Hollerton Silver Band?

9   The year Tony Blair's Labour government came to power, who had to leave Ambridge in a hurry after abusing Shula and Debbie?

10   Incriminating fingerprints were found on which object when an Ambridge resident was suspected of the infamous Borchester mail van robbery?

11 In the mid 1980s, sprayed on the wall of the magistrates' court was a notification that someone wore thermal vests. Who supposedly favoured these warm undergarments?

12 Which of the Archer family suffered from myxoedema, and what is it? Was it Elizabeth and a form of word blindness, Thomas the rabbit and a virus causing fur loss, or Jill and a thyroid deficiency?

13 In the year the Abortion Act became law in England, Scotland and Wales, which unmarried Ambridge resident was determined to have her child?

14 David Archer and Brookfield received unwanted attention after David witnessed a brutal attack and was determined to give evidence in court. Whose attack did he witness?

15 After Mark Hebden's tragic death in 1994, a trophy was named in his honour. At which annual event is the Mark Hebden Memorial Trophy awarded?

16 When young, good-looking police officer Harrison Burns first visited Ambridge he came to deliver a talk to which Ambridge society?

17 After drowning his sorrows at The Bull, who was on his way to Grey Gables when he was hit by a car which appeared to be out of control and did not stop?

18 Always ready to turn to dubious schemes, which night of the year did Joe Grundy believe was the best for poaching and why?

19 When Matt ran out on Lilian taking the contents of their bank account and the safe with him, he left her a two-word note – which seems a bit inadequate under the circumstances. What did he write?

20 In the 1990s what role did an enterprising Kate Aldridge play in helping thwart the gun-wielding criminals who were threatening people in the village shop?

Home Farm

HOME FARM HOUSE is a substantial eighteenth-century pile, originally called Ambridge Court, but allegedly built on the foundations of the ancient Lyttleton Manor. When the Aldridges were forced to sell it, the purchasers did not immediately take up residence. A series of skips appeared outside, into which a quantity of household fixtures were dumped, including garden ornaments, and elements of Jennifer's much-prized kitchen. The family has now moved in, but have yet to make their mark on the Ambridge social scene. They do not frequent the pub, or the village shop, and not even Susan Carter appears to know anything about them.

As well as selling the house, Brian was forced to cede the management of the farm to his stepson, Adam, a move which in my opinion was long overdue. Home Farm under Brian's leadership was stuck in the twentieth century, the epitome of industrial farming, dependent on chemical fertilisers, pesticides and weedkillers. Happily, Adam, understanding the damage that decades of abuse have done to the soil, takes an infinitely more holistic approach.

He has instigated the no-till sowing of crops, planted deep-rooted herbs to improve the soil structure, and created herbal leys for cattle to graze and to encourage beneficial insect populations. Better late than never.

Meanwhile Adam's half-sister Kate has created a thriving 'wellness' business. Her family have been somewhat dismissive of this. Indeed, when Brian was casting around for the means to pay for the clean-up, he proposed selling the piece of land which adjoins Kate's establishment. The consequent movement of tractors and heavy machinery would have completely destroyed the tranquil ambience which is fundamental to its entire ethos. Kate dug in her heels, and, quite rightly, forced Brian to change tack. I have a lot of time for Kate. Yes, she is eccentric, and has had a somewhat chequered past, but with this enterprise she has truly tapped into the zeitgeist, and should be applauded. I myself once toyed with the idea of becoming an aromatherapist.

Speaking of which, don't forget to sniff out the answers to the accumulator as you complete the quiz. Look at the answer to question 13. You need the first letter of the first word.

THE FULL MONTY

1   What name was given to Kate's business, which she
    runs from Home Farm? Was it Home from Home,
    No Place Like Home or Spiritual Home?

2   Which important occasion came first in Brian
    Aldridge's life: was it his wedding to Jennifer or his
    purchase of Home Farm?

3   Brian has never been one to turn down a slap-up
    meal. Why did his taste for goulash increase in the
    early part of the new millennium?

4   Which statesman did Jazzer say Adam and Ian's son
    Xander looked like when he was born?

5   How do an organ of a fish, a liquid measure and a
    wooded ravine link to Home Farm?

THE RADIO CARTER

6 Who was unfaithful with a casual Polish strawberry picker called Pawel who was working at Home Farm?

7 Fidelity is not Brian's strong suit. He had been married to Jennifer for nine years when he began an extramarital affair with which Ambridge resident?

8 There are a number of surnames of children whose parents have lived or worked at Home Farm. There have been Aldridges, Madikanes and a Donovan to name but a few. With the arrival of baby Xander which other surname is added to the list?

9 What did feckless Toby Fairbrother pour into the Home Farm swimming pool to turn the water purple?

10 Jennifer was not married to the father of her son, Adam. Brian wasn't married to the mother of his son, Ruairi. Other than this lack of marital status what did those two people have in common?

11 After witnessing a scrap between Ed and Will Grundy what revelation prompted Adam to fire Ed from Home Farm?

THE PEGGY WOOLLEY

12 Which of his cleaning ladies at Home Farm did Brian proposition by suggesting they go skinny-dipping in Home Farm's swimming pool?

13 Who used the pseudonym A.C. Ragini to fix an appointment with a representative of Home Farm?

14 Where did Adam and Ian share their first kiss?

15 For a short time a craft studio ran at Home Farm called the Two Jays. Who were the two Jays?

16 Who said to Brian, 'You farmers. You just don't know you're born!'?

17 Which favourite pub dish was Sammy Whipple justly entitled to order?

THE JIM LLOYD

18 Which item led Debbie to realising Ruairi was her stepfather Brian's son?

19 Brian has found himself in some very tricky situations down the years. Why was 'Tricky' a disaster for him, which reached its peak in 2019?

20 What links a dinosaur, a spaceship and a wizard?

Willow Farm and Ambridge Hall

MOST OF THE Willow Farm land is now part of Brookfield, but the farmhouse was acquired by the Tucker family, and is still the residence of Roy Tucker, deputy manager of Grey Gables Hotel, and his daughter Phoebe. Roy's wife, Hayley, left him, taking their younger daughter, after an alleged infidelity on his part. I find this very hard to believe; I worked with Roy Tucker for many years, and he is a most honourable man.

The other residence on this site, the tiny Willow Cottage, is now occupied by Brian and Jennifer Aldridge.

I cannot deny feeling just the tiniest frisson of *Schadenfreude* at Jennifer's undoing. She took such extravagant pride in her pretentiously over-furnished home with its shiny state-of-the-art kitchen, its swimming pool and oh-so-perfectly manicured gardens. She was, remember, a publican's daughter who gave birth to an illegitimate child back in the day when such things were frowned upon. I suppose that is why she, apparently willingly, took on the raising of Brian's illegitimate offspring, Ruairi Donovan. Brian owes her an eternal debt of gratitude for that. And expecting her, on top of that, to sacrifice her beloved home . . . Well, if I were in her shoes, I think I should have given Brian his marching orders. All that being said, one can only admire the fortitude with which Jennifer tolerates such severely reduced circumstances.

What the Aldridges should have done, in my opinion, was to follow the example set by me and Robert when we suffered an unfortunate setback in our lives. Welcome to Ambridge Hall!

As you can see our home is a handsome and substantial yellow brick house, built in the 1860s by the Lawson-Hope family. It has six bedrooms, not including the servants' quarters in the attic, so we decided to make the house pay its way, and opened it as a bed and breakfast for discerning guests. As well as offering all the pleasures of the countryside, our guests may enjoy home-cooked breakfasts featuring entirely local produce, access to my extensive low-allergen garden (a great boon for those, like me, afflicted with hay fever), and the company of my two delightful and very friendly llamas. There is a traditional shepherd's hut in my garden, built for me by Eddie Grundy. However the interior is a space Robert and

I prefer to keep for private meditation, and so is not open to visitors.

Once you've finished perusing my garden and have answered the questions I've set, look at the answer to question 11. You need the first letter of the first word.

THE FULL MONTY

1 When Lynda hosted a Victorian Christmas at Ambridge Hall, which meat was the centrepiece of the meal?

2 This couple have spent more time in mobile homes than the average member of the Caravan Club. In 2005 they found themselves at Willow Farm. Who were they?

3 One of Robert Snell's daughters has a herb-linked name. Is she called Coriander, Rosemary or Sorrel?

4 Who vanished on the night of the floods but returned on Christmas Eve the same year?

5 In which Ambridge property did the Snells take up temporary residence after the floods of 2015?

THE RADIO CARTER

6   Lynda once innocently lent a cricket book to another villager. She hadn't realised that an early love letter Robert had sent her had been left inside the book, revealing the private nickname he used to sign off the note. What name did he use?

7   With which member of the Archer family did Roy Tucker have an affair, which cost him his marriage?

8   The rooms at Ambridge Hall have been planned by Lynda in accordance with the practice of Chinese geomancy. How is Chinese geomancy better known?

9   How was Mike Tucker's second wife Vicky well placed professionally to bring a smile to his face, and what was her nickname for him?

10   Why might Francis Winterbury and Lynda have exchanged a considerable degree of correspondence by letter?

11   Jennifer was adamant she would keep the family together after selling Home Farm. The downsizing move to Willow Cottage took her and Brian closer to which granddaughter?

THE PEGGY WOOLLEY

12 Visiting the Birmingham Hippodrome, Lynda became involved in audience/performer banter with which megastar?

13 Ambridge Hall was originally built for a person who carried out a specific job. Since then many other people have taken on this role, but none have lived at the hall in recent years. What is the job in question?

14 Literature and gardening are two of Lynda's great passions. From which literary figure has she drawn inspiration when choosing which flowers to plant in her garden?

15 Back in 2008, what major building project was undertaken at Willow Farm?

16 Griff Rhys Jones was drafted in to support Lynda's campaign to restore what to the area?

17 In 2007, which world-famous fertility specialist advised Roy and Hayley Tucker?

THE JIM LLOYD

18 A prime number is a whole number greater than one, which can be divided by one and by itself but not by any other number. Which prime number is special for Lynda?

19 What's the link between Ambridge Hall and the musician who declared himself 'the patron saint of mediocrities'?

20 Prior to her accident at Grey Gables, what specialist course had Lynda signed up for?

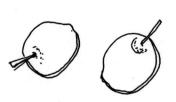

AM-GRAM

Rearrange the letters to make the name of an
Ambridge resident. There is a clue to help you.
The answer appears at the foot of the page.

BORN TELLERS

Nothing to do with stories or banks.

Grey Gables and The Lodge

NOW WE COME to what was until very recently my place of work, The Grey Gables Hotel. It was originally built in 1898 as a country house, designed by Benjamin Perry for industrialist George Gibbins of Gibbins and Bromyard, iron founders in Birmingham. It is Grade II listed as a prime example of brick neo-Gothic. Twenty-four of the hotel's sixty bedrooms are in the main house, and there are in addition a ballroom, several function rooms and of course a highly rated restaurant. When Robert and I first arrived in Ambridge, the hotel had the somewhat fustian atmosphere of a gentlemen's club.

But then Caroline was appointed manager. She was a breath of fresh air, and the place was transformed. It was she who introduced the health club and swimming pool, a great boon to local residents, as well as hotel guests. Caroline subsequently married Oliver, and they bought the hotel from its previous owner. Oliver still owns it, but darling Caroline is alas no longer with us.

You will no doubt be aware that Grey Gables was in the news not so very long ago, when parts of the building were destroyed by an explosion. I was unfortunately a victim of that event, which is why I no longer work there. However, as you may observe, I am well on the road to recovery.

As we walk back up to the main road, we pass a black-and-white timbered building, which is the home of Peggy Woolley. Her life is a real rags-to-riches story. Born Peggy Perkins in the East End of London, she joined the ATS during the war when she met and married a member of the Archer family. They returned to Ambridge, where he was landlord of The Bull, and where they brought up their three children, Jennifer, Lilian and Tony. After her first husband's death, Peggy became PA to Mr Woolley at Grey Gables, and married him in 1991.

Now widowed, and in her nineties, Peggy still plays a significant role in village life, most recently having devoted a large part of her considerable wealth to establishing the Ambridge Conservation Trust. Too many of the older generation care more about their gas-guzzling cars and foreign holidays than about the future of the planet. Peggy is an inspiration to us all.

To find another letter of the accumulator, look at the answer to question 3. You need the first letter of the first word.

THE FULL MONTY

1   In 2020, in which room did a catastrophic explosion occur at Grey Gables?

2   The _ _ _ _ _ Garden Suite. What word will complete the name of the hotel's most prestigious set of rooms?

3   Which of the Woolley clan shares her name with a tree?

4   Grey Gables' Arkwright Room was developed to provide which facility? Was it a conference room, a fine dining area or a health spa?

5   Which outdoor leisure facility did Jack Woolley introduce to Grey Gables in the early 1960s?

THE RADIO CARTER

6 In preparation for Will and Nic's wedding, what needed a desperate eleventh-hour repair before the big event? Was it the cake, the car or the dress?

7 Tracy Horrobin observed a man through the window and was horrified to see what looked like blood all over his face. In fact it was something much less alarming. What was it?

8 What did a Mrs Jones, who was staying in room number thirteen, complain about during her stay at Grey Gables in 2019?

9 Why did Christine Barford move out of The Lodge? Did she have a fall, did she fall out with her 'housemate' Peggy or could she no longer afford to stay there after she lost money through bad investment?

10 The incongruous quartet of Grey Gables owner Oliver Sterling, Robert Snell, Jazzer McCreary and Baggy are linked by which association?

11 After bagging the prize of a weekend for two at Grey Gables at the Flower and Produce Show, who tried to claim half the cost of the weekend in cash?

THE PEGGY WOOLLEY

12 Grace Archer died rescuing a horse from the burning stables at Grey Gables. What was the horse called and how was it she discovered the fire?

13 Higgs was a devoted employee of Jack Woolley's. What did he do?

14 It's hardly *Fifty Shades of Grey*, but apart from Grey Gables what other Grey named item was owned by Jack Woolley?

15 In the 1980s, which famous lady attended a fashion show at Grey Gables in connection with the centenary of the NSPCC?

16 Head chef Jean Paul never got to ice Susan and Neil Carter's wedding cake. What unusual occurrence stopped him doing so?

17 Which radio station held its annual Christmas dinner at Grey Gables back in 1991? Was it Radio Borsetshire, Felpersham Hospital Radio, Radio 1 or Radio 4?

THE JIM LLOYD

18 Caroline had a long relationship with Grey Gables. She had three different surnames when she lived in and around Ambridge. Which surname contained the greatest number of letters?

19 With declining health, what terrified and confused Jack Woolley and made him think the Second World War was still continuing?

20 After the catastrophic explosion there, which facility at Grey Gables was allowed to reopen on 13 May 2020?

Reflections:
What's in a Name?

LET US PAUSE a while, take advantage of these deckchairs by the cricket ground, and see what you can make of some fiendishly cryptic questions and word-based puzzles inspired by the names of people and places in Ambridge.

1   Which larger than life former Ambridge resident shared a first name with a military leader who is honoured with a central London monument?

2   What is the Ambridge link with a cake, a town in Greater Manchester and a surreal radio comedy of the 1950s and 1960s?

3   Dylan Nells is the pen name of which scribe of Ambridge?

4   Who or what was Primrose Bank? Was it a field at Bridge Farm, the name of Joe Grundy's very first girlfriend or an offshore investment scam set up by Simon Pemberton?

5   When they returned from a honeymoon in Mexico what did Will and Emma Grundy name their house? Did they call it Aztec Horizons, Casa Nueva or Tequila Sunrise?

6 When Will Grundy married Nic, what did he rename their home?

7 Which Archer's first name of three letters has two anagrams?

8 When Peggy Perkins first came to Ambridge, little did she know that she would marry – twice. Can you name both her husbands?

9 In Ambridge place names what word can follow Grange, Green and Pheasant?

10 Whose first name contains a letter E and the Roman numerals for 61?

11   What word links Friends and Sisters in the names of very different Borsetshire eateries?

12   Which girls' comic first published in 1958 shares its name with Mark Hebden's mother?

13   Certain letters of the alphabet when written as capitals have mirror symmetry. The left half of the letter mirrors the right and vice versa. The letter X is an example. Which of the Archer clan has a first name made up of letters which all have mirror symmetry as capital letters?

14   Ambridge Court was once a large building divided into individual flats. What name did it take after its restoration to a graceful manor house?

15   Which two Ambridge married couples over the years have the least number of letters in their combined first names?

16   Sometimes you need to think outside the box to
solve a question. Sometimes you need to think
about the box itself. Which Archer first name forms a
special link with the words, DUET, EDEN and UNDO?

17   At first glance, Ambridge residents Christopher,
Marjorie and Ruairi would seem to have nothing in
common. They were different ages, had different
backgrounds and had different aspirations. However,
when you look at their full names there is a moving
link. What is it?

18   At whose wedding was the witness – quite literally –
an absolute Brick?

19   What does Tumble Tussock give its name to?

20   Larry Lovell can confirm that Neil Diamond has
never visited Borsetshire. However his song titles
do by chance namecheck Borsetshire folk and a
Borsetshire location. There's a Sweet lady, a Pretty
Amazing lady and a Cracklin' (young) lady. Who
are they? And which Neil Diamond composition
pays reference in its title to a prominent feature in
Ambridge?

The Cricket Pavilion and The Village Hall

AH, THE CRICKET pavilion. My husband Robert was for many years a member of the team, so I have from time to time sat here on a summer afternoon, watching Ambridge struggle to maintain their place in the Village Cricket League, without having any particular grasp of the rules. However, all that changed recently when a new kind of challenge was introduced to quiz nights at The Bull. It is called Beat the Brainboxes, a team of superior Ambridge intellects, for which I was selected, presumably because of my extensive knowledge of literature and the theatre. However, I was somewhat embarrassingly defeated when pitted against Eddie Grundy in the sports round. So I resolved to plug this gap in my knowledge by studying the laws of cricket. And I was thus able to identify a no-ball in a crucial game between Ambridge and their arch-rivals, Darrington. Unfortunately, however, the subject of cricket has never again come up in the Beat the Brainboxes sports round.

Let us move on to our next venue, the village hall. I became involved in amateur dramatics at our previous home in Sunningdale, and recognised what a wonderful way it is to bring a community together. As any drama teacher will tell you, it is an activity that stimulates the imagination, and promotes teamwork and communication skills. And such qualities were much in evidence when the village hall was severely damaged in the 2015 flood, and in need of restoration. It was a stirring speech by Eddie Grundy that galvanised the residents into action. (I take some credit for teaching Eddie how to project, having directed him in several Christmas shows.) And teamwork was very much in evidence, as dozens of villagers rallied round to rebuild, redecorate and refurbish the hall. I contributed the profits from that year's Christmas show, which had had to relocate to Lower Loxley, to the renovation cause. It was an enormous pleasure to return to the wonderfully rejuvenated hall the following Christmas with my production of *Mother Goose*.

Has the accumulator left you 'stumped' (my little joke)? Look at the answer to question 2. You need the first letter of the first word.

THE FULL MONTY

1   Who went head-to-head for the captaincy of the cricket team prior to the 2020 season?

2   Despite Lynda's persuasive tongue, who has she not coerced into playing the pantomime dame? Is it Neil Carter, Nigel Pargetter or Mike Tucker?

3   In which month of the year is the single wicket competition usually held?

4   In which vital role at the cricket club did Fallon take over from Shula?

5   Typecast? Who took on the role of the curmudgeonly miser Ebenezer Scrooge in Lynda's version of the Charles Dickens classic, *A Christmas Carol*?

THE RADIO CARTER

6   Which genuine Archer played a fictional archer in a village production?

7   Jean Harvey was the overall winner of the Flower and Produce Show in 1977. She repeated the triumph the following year but was then disqualified. Why?

8   Which famous TV presenter returned to Ambridge for a second visit to open the village hall after its post-flood refurbishment?

9   How did Average and Shorty find fame at the village hall? Were they country and western friends of Jolene, pantomime characters or rabbits in the favourite pet section at the Summer Fete?

10   How did membership of the village cricket team change in 2017?

11   Was it the village hall or the cricket pavilion which was named after a former owner of the *Borchester Echo*?

THE PEGGY WOOLLEY

12 In 2015, Lynda had to find an alternative location for her Christmas show, as the village hall was still flood-damaged. The show revealed more bare flesh than previous Lynda Snell productions. Was it *The Full Monty*, *Calendar Girls* or *Lady Chatterley's Lover*?

13 The village hall was originally used as what? Was it the blacksmith's forge, the courthouse or the village school?

14 In a shocking incident, Owen King raped Kathy Perks following a play rehearsal. Understandably Kathy felt unable to carry on with the show, but what was the production and what part was Kathy set to play?

15 At a cricket club meeting who said, 'We all know why Dr Locke left Ambridge and it had nothing to do with cricket,' whereupon Shula fled from the room?

16 In the inaugural single wicket competition which Ambridge lady faced John Archer in the final round, only to miss out on victory when her husband kicked his ball over a boundary?

17 To draw attention to inequality around the world, Caroline persuaded then fiancé Robin Stokes to have a 'rich man, poor man' theme at the annual harvest supper. Diners took pot luck as to which category they fell into. True to type, Brian was served a hearty casserole. What did Joe Grundy receive?

THE JIM LLOYD

18 At the Flower and Produce Show, the trophy for overall achievement is named in honour of which late Ambridge resident?

19 Which play directed by Lynda includes the characters Dr & Mrs Bradman and a maid called Edith? Which work by the same playwright might she have avoided due to one of her underlying health issues?

20 In entertainment circles many people take great pride in saying they are members of FLOPS. What does FLOPS stand for?

Blossom Hill
Cottage

ON OUR WAY out of the village we pass Blossom Hill Cottage, a picture-book little residence, which was for many years home to the widowed Peggy Archer, before she became Mrs Woolley. And before that, so I'm told, it was occupied by Peggy's mother, an East End matron known locally as Mrs P. Neither of these ladies was troubled with anything more sinister than the occasional rat. But in recent times, this house has witnessed some truly disturbing events.

After her second marriage, Peggy sold the cottage to Usha Gupta, as she then was. Although Usha received a warm welcome from the vast majority of villagers, there were a few, a very few, bigoted young men who subjected her to a campaign of harassment, and ended up assaulting Usha and trashing the cottage. I am happy to report that the perpetrators were brought to justice, that Usha overcame her understandable subsequent qualms, and continued to live here in peace and tranquillity, until she fell in love and married our local vicar, Alan Franks.

But as many of you will be aware, this house has witnessed an even more infamous series of events. It was here that Helen Archer, daughter of Tony and Pat, came to live with her husband Rob Titchener. The outwardly charming Mr Titchener turned out to be not so charming after all, but a controlling bully who drove poor Helen to such extremes that she finally snapped, attacked him with a kitchen knife, was tried, convicted and sent to prison. Happily the conviction was quashed, and Helen emerged from her ordeal strong and resolute.

The reason the front hedge is so high, Usha tells me, is to deter sightseers, who, after all the publicity surrounding the case, came to gawp at the scene of the crime. As a result, she had considerable difficulty finding new tenants for the cottage.

Do you have your pens at the ready? Look at the answer to question 2. You need the first letter of the first word.

THE FULL MONTY

1   Some cottages are small, some are quite large; how many bedrooms are there in Blossom Hill Cottage? Are there two, three or six?

2   It sounds like a picture-postcard traditional building. Is the roof made of red tile, slate or thatch?

3   A solicitor owns Blossom Hill Cottage, but lives at the vicarage. What's her name?

4   How did Anna Tregorran feature after the stabbing at Blossom Hill Cottage?

5   In which room in the cottage did Helen stab Rob?

THE RADIO CARTER

6 For what was Helen sent to prison? Was it grievous bodily harm, possession of an offensive weapon or attempted murder?

7 What had Rob threatened when Helen first said she would kill him? Was it because he said they were going to live overseas, he was going to send Henry to boarding school or he was going to have her sectioned?

8 What specific event was Rob referring to when he said in court, 'I've never regretted anything more in my life.'?

9 Who said the words, 'He's breathing,' after it was thought Rob had breathed his last?

10 What did Rob use as an excuse to prevent Helen from driving her car? Was it because she was heavily pregnant, she had had a minor car accident or she had inadvertently put the wrong fuel in the tank?

11 What foodstuff was splattered over the walls after the stabbing?

THE PEGGY WOOLLEY

12   John Tregorran and Carol Grenville eventually got together in the late 1960s. Between them they owned Blossom Hill Cottage and which other Ambridge property?

13   In the early days of television, in the 1950s, the squire offered tenant Mike Daly the use of a TV set. Why was this of no use to Mike at the time?

14   Why did Peggy move temporarily out of Blossom Hill Cottage to Home Farm? Was it because she thought it was haunted, Blossom Hill Cottage had been damaged by fire or there was an infestation of wasps? And who moved with her?

15   Why was Dr Locke shocked when he called to collect his furniture at Usha's house prior to leaving for a new job in Manchester?

16   Roger Travers-Macy and wife Jennifer were perhaps ahead of their time. As tenants at Blossom Hill Cottage in the late 1960s did they use it as a buy to let, a holiday cottage or a weekend retreat for themselves?

17   Which classic car enthusiast had a short stay at Blossom Hill Cottage when he first came to Ambridge?

THE JIM LLOYD

18 What is the link between playwright Patrick Hamilton and events at Blossom Hill Cottage?

19 How did members of the Scombridae family cause a series of unpleasant incidents at Blossom Hill Cottage?

20 A teacher, a veterinary surgeon, a solicitor, a spy, a plumber and a university professor. Which of these has NOT been a Blossom Hill cottage owner or tenant?

Lower Loxley

FINALLY, WE ALIGHT at Lower Loxley, ancestral home of
the Pargetter family. The date above the front door is
1702, but the family tree can be traced back even earlier
– it is said there have been Pargetters in the area since
the sixteenth century. The house is Grade II listed and
boasts a ballroom with spectacular chandeliers, a beautiful
neoclassical drawing room and library, and at the top of
the house, in the old nursery and servants' quarters, a
charming toy museum. Outside there are three acres of
formal garden, a seven-acre arboretum, as well as extensive
parkland to the front and rear. The house and gardens are
open to the public, and I can wholeheartedly recommend
the café in the Orangery.

Elizabeth Archer worked as marketing manager for the
estate, and married Nigel Pargetter in 1994. But as you may
be aware, Nigel died in a freak accident, falling from the roof.
He was a great loss, and not just to his family. His penchant
for dressing up as a gorilla and playing practical jokes could
be regarded as puerile, but he was a genuine eccentric,
which, one gathers, is something of a Pargetter trait.

Since his death, his widow Elizabeth has kept the business afloat, whilst bringing up her children, Lily and Freddie. To say this has not gone smoothly is something of an understatement. Freddie is heir to the estate, quite unjustly in my opinion, the tradition of male primogeniture being wholly inappropriate in this day and age. And frankly, his sister Lily, a very bright young woman, is infinitely more suited to the management of such a substantial business. However, Lily became involved with a married tutor at her sixth-form college, and subsequently dropped out of university. She and the aforementioned tutor returned to Lower Loxley, where he pursues his, so far unsuccessful, ambition to become a famous artist, while she wastes her substantial gifts selling kitchens. Meanwhile her brother Freddie was arrested for drug dealing and spent six months in a young offender institution. That was the straw that broke the camel's back for poor Elizabeth, who had soldiered on so bravely since her husband's death.

But the fact that I am here today I owe to Freddie Pargetter, who dragged me from the wreckage after the Grey Gables explosion, and to his mother, Elizabeth, who showed me that it is possible to recover from trauma and depression. I shall be eternally in their debt.

When you have finished cogitating over my questions on Lower Loxley, you should have collected all the letters needed to spell out the hidden message. Look at the answer to question 17. You need the first letter of the third word. Once you have found this, rearrange your fifteen letters into a five-letter word and a ten-letter word. Good luck!

THE FULL MONTY

1   Who was with Nigel Pargetter when he fell to his death from the roof of his family home?

2   Held usually but not exclusively at Lower Loxley in late October, which produce gets its own fun day, with various events and attractions?

3   Part of the Lower Loxley attractions, were the Derbyshire Redcaps rare breed hens or touring baseball players?

4   What was the profession of Jamila, an important figure to a Lower Loxley resident?

5   Inspired by his eccentric Great-Great-Uncle Edmund, who was a phenologist, Nigel became quite the eco-warrior. He even started to host green weddings at Lower Loxley. Mindful of both the environment and cost, what was thrown as an alternative to confetti at these weddings?

THE RADIO CARTER

6 Madeleine Angevine played an important part in developments at Lower Loxley with the approval of Nigel and Elizabeth. Who or what was Madeleine Angevine?

7 After his release from the young offender institution, Freddie realised that something could not come back if he remained at Lower Loxley. What was it?

8 In 2006, Nigel caught a chill after swimming across Lower Loxley lake dressed as which romantic hero?

9 At a Lower Loxley beer festival, Harrison Burns made an arrest while dressed as which Spice Girl?

10 During a meeting with a senior tutor at college, what did Freddie notice that convinced him his own sister was having an affair?

11 Nigel appeared at Lizzie's hen do wearing his gorilla suit, but how had Debbie and Usha outmonkeyed him?

THE PEGGY WOOLLEY

12 How did Cranford Crystal play a significant part at Nigel's funeral?

13 Which tool appears on the Pargetter coat of arms?

14 Nigel had a nanny who used to tell him that the stone gryphons could come to life and do what?

15 In the early noughties what did Elizabeth find flying from the Lower Loxley flagpole as she was preparing to greet a group of bank managers for a conference?

16 Rehearsals were under way for a performance at Lower Loxley when news broke that Princess Diana had died in a car crash. Which play was it?

17 What totally inappropriate three-word message was on the banner that Nigel was attempting to remove when he fell from the roof?

THE JIM LLOYD

18 Bunbury is a special character in the play *The Importance of Being Earnest* by Oscar Wilde. Who was the Lower Loxley equivalent?

19 What links one of the more infamous careers of Nigel Pargetter and a Belgian reporter and detective?

20 Kenton Archer and Shula Hebden-Lloyd share a similarity with their nephew and niece Lily and Freddie Pargetter. What is it?

Reflections:
None of
Your Business

FINALLY, LET US rest our weary legs here in the lovely Lower Loxley gardens, and tackle one last selection of questions. The people of Ambridge are an enterprising bunch, and the focus on this section is on their many and varied careers, pastimes and money-making schemes.

1   Natasha made a success of her business Summer
    Orchard. What was the business concerned with?
    Was it cosmetics, fruit drinks or tree surgery?

2   Neil Carter and Josh Archer have both set up a
    business dealing with which farm produce?

3   Did Shula describe her interview at the selection
    process to train for the priesthood as 'Worse than
    The Apprentice', 'Worse than *Mastermind*' or 'Worse
    than *Dragons' Den*'?

4   How was Janet Fisher an Ambridge pioneer?

5   Many folk in Ambridge work hard, but who combined
    night shifts in a chicken factory, a cleaning job by
    day and working at the Tearoom, while still bringing
    up young children?

6   Which budding musician had a band called Little White Lies? Was it David Archer, Eddie Grundy or Fallon Rogers?

7   'Wise Words with Wendy' is the *Westbury Courier*'s salacious advice column. Which Ambridge resident moonlights as Wendy the agony aunt?

8   Richard Adamson and Matthew Wreford held which post in Ambridge? Were they farm managers, postmen or vicars?

9   Leonard Berry, Jim Lloyd and Richard Locke all have slightly unusual hobbies outside of their illustrious professional work. Match the hobbies to the individuals. a) English Civil War recreation, b) hot air ballooning and c) magic tricks.

10   On his retirement from farming which of Phil Archer's new hobbies did his wife Jill find particularly annoying?

11 What did would-be sausage king Tom Archer call his food van? Was it The Banger Bus, Gourmet Grills or The Hot G'rilla?

12 Martha Woodford, Usha Gupta, Laura Archer and Lynda Snell have all taken on which imaginative role at the Ambridge Fete?

13 Is there anyone still farming in Ambridge as the United Kingdom leaves the EU, who was farming at their own farm in Ambridge when it joined the Common Market on 1 January 1973?

14 What was C3PL? Was it a company with Matt Crawford as a director, a robot from Jazzer's favourite computer game or a form of software developed by Robert Snell?

15 Practice makes perfect, according to the saying. What did Tim Hathaway practise in Ambridge?

16 Lily Pargetter met her boyfriend Russ Jones through college, though he wasn't there as a student. Eyebrows were raised over their difference in age. Is it about ten years, about fifteen years or about twenty years?

17 'Maybe they'll give me a smock and a pitchfork and stick me in a museum: British farmer, extinct.' Who said these words? Was it Brian Aldridge, David Archer or Eddie Grundy?

18 Dave Barry's job sent him all over Ambridge. Was he a gamekeeper, a police officer or a tree surgeon?

19 Which Ambridge singer used to be known as the Lily of Layton Cross?

20 In her younger days Shula worked for the agents Rodway and Watson's. Were they estate agents, secret agents or travel agents?

AM-GRAM

Rearrange the letters to make the name of an
Ambridge resident. There is a clue to help you.
The answer appears at the foot of the page.

I LABEL MANY ILL

But I've a heart of gold, darling!

Answer: LILIAN BELLAMY

SOLUTIONS

Lakey Hill

1. The Malverns.

2. April Cottage. Back in the sixties, this cottage was built by Charles Grenville as part of a pair with Keeper's Cottage. It's occupied by Kathy and Jamie Perks.

3. Kent. It appears in Kenton: stuck on what name to give their eldest son, Phil and Jill got out some alphabet building blocks and threw them into the air!

4. Brookfield. Lakey Hill belongs to David and Ruth's place of work and their family home.

5. Easter Day. The early birds in attendance then walk down to the village hall where breakfast is served.

6. Kate Aldridge and Roy Tucker, parents of Phoebe.
    She was named after her great-great-great-
    grandmother. Prior to the ceremony, Phoebe had
    spent three months nameless, during which time
    Kate had tried to abscond to France with her and
    Roy had had to prove his paternity with a DNA test!

7. Phil Archer. He was asking his wife Jill after
    storming out of Brookfield to escape her noisy
    B&B guests. Jill's guests kept her so busy that
    she struggled to find time for Phil, until their
    daughter-in-law Ruth orchestrated their reunion
    on Lakey Hill.

8. Emma Grundy. She eventually chose Keira as
    Clarrie talked her out of 'Scarlett'.

9. George Barford. He had suffered a fatal heart attack
    but his dog Walt remained at his master's side.

10. Alistair Lloyd proposed to Shula Hebden née Archer.
    She was so taken aback that Alistair had to keep hold
    of the ring and wait five days for her to accept.

11. Elizabeth Archer. She was having a heart-to-heart
    with her father, Phil.

12. A bonfire and fireworks. The date was 2 June 1953 and

Phil Archer and Grace Fairbrother stayed out celebrating until 4 a.m. They got engaged the following year.

13. Afghan hounds. At one point, Marjorie had eight of them, whom she lovingly referred to as her 'girls'.

14. Woodbine Cottage. Nigel Pargetter was having a house-warming celebration after renting the property from Phil Archer.

15. They had lost their first baby due to an ectopic pregnancy.

16. Bank Farm, home to Ron and Vera Medlar.

17. He started fires indiscriminately. He was a pyromaniac and was eventually committed to hospital. A beacon was lit for the golden jubilee – Frank would have approved of the fiery display.

18. Lakey Hill. It rises to 771 feet. Blackpool Tower is 519 feet. The London Eye is 443 feet.

19. Two. There's Green Farm and Red House Farm. Sadly there isn't an Amber-idge Farm!

20. Kale. The four letters in kale can be found in the name Lakey Hill.

The Bull

1. Matt Crawford. Lilian's pet name for him was Tiger.

2. She was the cook. Her cooking was the stuff of legend, particularly her pies!

3. The B @ Ambridge.

4. No. It's Nightingale Farm.

5. Bella. She was a barmaid who left The Bull in 2020 after breaking Johnny Phillips' heart.

6. Doreen. All together now . . . Doreen, Doreen, Doreen, Dor-ee-ee-een, I'm begging of you please don't take my man!

7. Justin Elliott proposed to Lilian. In the end they decided to live together without the formalities of a recognised wedding ceremony. The following year, Harrison took over the microphone after the pub quiz and very publicly proposed to Fallon.

8. Jamie Perks. Jamie would have been Kenton's stepson if Kenton had previously married long-term partner Kathy Perks.

9. He was a ghost hunter. Lucy Perks was hearing strange noises at The Bull and Ted was called in to investigate.

10. He was found to have ice cubes in his pocket, which he used to numb his mouth. This was felt to be an unfair advantage.

11. Jolene Perks. They had been married for three years.

12. He is a peacock.

13. Husband Jack Archer was discovered serving alcohol after hours and therefore could not continue as the licensee.

14. Guy Pemberton.

15. Clarrie Larkin. The year was 1981 and she married Eddie Grundy. His initial proposal to Clarrie was interrupted when Jolene phoned to ask Eddie to make a music tape with her. He finally proposed in the September of that year and they were married two months later.

16. A milk tanker. Polly had been on her way to the cash and carry with Pat Archer, who was unharmed.

17. Jack was never told. He was suffering from Alzheimer's and his wife Peggy felt it better not to confuse or worry him. Sid's introduction to Ambridge came in the early sixties when he stayed at Grey Gables. Though Sid was a stark contrast to the usual clientele, Jack saw potential in the fellow Brummie and took him under his wing.

18. The Wars of the Roses (fifteenth century).

19. Both were involved in a scandalous event in a shower. Jolene Rogers and Sid Perks splashed about together, and later were married. In the movie Psycho, Janet Leigh's character, Marion Crane, was not so fortunate. She was slashed to death in a shower room at the Bates Motel.

20. They all have! There are some impossible scores in darts with three arrows. David's 166 is one; Neil's 163 is impossible, as is Eddie's 172. Give it a go if you are not sure – and go easy on the Shires.

The Village Green

1.   The Green is triangular.

2.   The Village Fete. This is usually in July or August, with the Flower and Produce Show following in September.

3.   The village shop. This vital source of newspapers and gossip was threatened with closure in 2015 when Hazel Woolley wanted to convert the whole building into flats. Master negotiator Peggy Woolley talked her round.

4.   St Stephen. St Stephen's Church and St Stephen's Day.

5.   Beauty. True countryman Walter Gabriel was an Ambridge stalwart in his day. Walter was a great friend of Peggy's mother, Mrs Perkins.

6.   A birthday party. It was Jim's own birthday and the event had been organised as a surprise for him.

7.   Alan Titchmarsh. Lynda still has nightmares about him catching her coaxing her pansies to bloom with a hairdryer.

8.   Freddie Pargetter. His plan to move out of The Stables, where he had been living with his Auntie Shula, and into a house share with his friend Johnny, was thwarted when he was caught up in an explosion at Grey Gables in early 2020. His mother Elizabeth insisted that he move home to Lower Loxley to recuperate.

9.   Decaffeinated coffee.

10. The Andrews Sisters. Kenton was such a fan of his outfit that he put it on long before the performance and wandered around in it.

11. Polly won £1000 on a premium bond, enough to put down a deposit on the village shop and post office.

12. It was destroyed by a fire when ne'er-do-well Clive Horrobin threw a petrol bomb through the window. David heard the commotion from The Bull and rushed over to rescue Christine Barford (his aunt) and his mum Jill Archer who were inside.

13. Jack Woolley.

14. His eye. He could frequently be heard saying 'My eye!'

15. It was the shop's phone number.

16. The Fete was opened by *Angel of the North* sculptor, Antony Gormley. The year was 2009. Inspired by Gormley's plinth installation in Trafalgar Square, the village held its own plinth performances at the Fete. Joe went to extra effort as the Angel of Ambridge in the hope that Gormley would award him with a sculpture he could sell online. The prize was in fact a signed book of his artworks, which was won by Molly Button.

17. The village phone box. Martha had quite a shock when she went to clean it early one morning and discovered it chained shut with Nigel Pargetter sleeping inside. Nigel, who was only wearing silk boxer shorts, had been locked in there as a stag do prank.

18. The village playground.

19. The Bull. Your star sign is Taurus – The Bull!

20. Honeysuckle Cottage. It is home to Adam, Ian and their son Xander.

Reflections:
Out of Ambridge

1. The Laurels, a nursing home between Ambridge and Penny Hassett. Leonard worked there as a volunteer and Jill was visiting her sister-in-law, Christine.

2. The Blackberry Line. This line still has its own steam train.

3. Wales.

4. Sid Perks.

5. Hollerton Junction. In the sixties it was at risk of closure, but this didn't bother Walter Gabriel who had hoped to buy up the scrap.

6. Phoebe Aldridge. A remarkably relaxed Kate gave birth in a tepee accompanied by birthing partner Morwenna, a friend she met on the road.

7. Rob Titchener and his first wife Jess. Jess moved to Hampshire and Rob fled to Minneapolis.

8. Sid Perks and Jolene Rogers, who had just become the new Mrs Perks.

9. Hebden Bridge. It combines Mark Hebden and Bridge Farm.

10. A motorway service station. It was off the M40. Cameron excused himself and then secretly drove away in his Jaguar.

11. 1992.

12. Kate Madikane's. They are Noluthando and Sipho and live in Durban with their dad, Lucas.

13. A car park. Usha thought it was perfect, as it was the place where their relationship first began when he rescued her on his motorbike.

14. She was dressed as a French maid.

15. The Dirty Duck. There is a pub called The Goat and Nightgown in the area too.

16. She went to Costa Rica with her housemate Rachel.

17. 'Roses of Picardy' was written by Haydn Wood. Heydon Wood is an area south of Ambridge.

18. Phil and Jill's golden wedding celebrations in 2008 and Phil's funeral in 2010. Carol finally returned to live in Ambridge in 2014 after the death of her husband, John.

19. France. They were looking to move to Normandy.

20. German. His mother Siobhan was an interpreter and they lived in Germany.

St Stephen's Church

1. Felpersham, which has a well-regarded cathedral school. Dan Hebden Lloyd, Lily and Freddie Pargetter and Ruairi Donovan have all been pupils there.

2. A campanologist (a bell-ringer). Neil and Chris Carter are both keen campanologists. A philatelist collects stamps. A numismatist collects coins.

3. Ruth.

4. Phil Archer. Valda replaced him as the church organist and she, in turn, was replaced by Patrick. In 2019, equine vet and accomplished musician Jakob volunteered to accompany Rosie Archer's christening. Much to her embarrassment, Shula told everyone that Jakob had 'grown up playing with a very impressive organ'.

5. The vestry. Tom realised on the day that he couldn't go through with the wedding and jilted a distraught Kirsty as soon as she arrived at the church.

6. Neil Carter. His wife Susan was jailed for protecting her feckless brother, Clive Horrobin.

7. She was a woman. Peggy strongly disapproved of the principle of women priests. For a while she worshipped at a different church.

8. Lord Patrick Lichfield.

9. A Fabergé egg. Lynda's glory of winning 'best costume' was dampened when she had to be cut out of it. The whole event was caught by the photographer from the *Borchester Echo* and a picture was published in the paper of Lynda in her underwear after being cut free.

10. A performance of Handel's *Messiah*. Shula had been singing as part of a scratch choir who turned up on the day to rehearse and performed that evening.

11. A 1970s bungalow.

12. John Archer's funeral. Hayley, his ex-girlfriend, introduced the music.

13. Grace, late wife of Philip Archer. He was married to his second wife, Jill, for almost fifty-three years

until his death. The window brought up some conflicting feelings for Jill, who admitted she sometimes wanted to put a brick through it.

14. She was dressed as a chicken, following a £500 bet with a colleague. Alan came to her rescue on discovering her car had been bashed into and their relationship gradually blossomed from that day on.

15. New toilets.

16. He died at Glebe Cottage. The music playing was Sir Edward Elgar's *The Dream of Gerontius*.

17. Brian (Aldridge) shares his name with Brian the Snail.

18. Bats. As a protected species it was a challenge to move them out of the church.

19. Robin Stokes, who was a vet as well as a vicar (unpaid). Baby Spice, Posh Spice and Ginger Spice were cows owned by the Grundys.

20. Shrove Tuesday. The event was a pancake-tossing competition, and then he had a four-mile hike to the pub for the rest of the festivities.

Grange Farm

1. George Barford, who mentored Will in his gamekeeping career and died just a few months before Emma gave birth to baby George.

2. Cider drinking. He spent a happy night with the Cider Club 'keeping the great Grundy traditions alive' with a cider pressing. Joe and the club also went to the liberty of drinking the remains of the previous year's cider.

3. Fat. He is known as Fat Paul. The Fat Controller is in the *Thomas the Tank Engine* stories.

4. Little Grange.

5. She had a sewing bee at her mother Susan Carter's house to make wedding decorations.

6. A flat in Meadow Rise and a caravan (illegally parked of course!).

7. Marjorie Antrobus.

8. Eddie played the same role in two different

productions at the same date and time. Both
Lynda and Bert pitched versions of *Aladdin* to
the village hall committee. Bert's was chosen,
so Lynda set up a rival production. Eddie had to
rush between Ambridge Hall and the village hall
on the night and, despite muddling his lines from
each performance, was considered the star of
both of the shows.

9. The family bath inside Grange Farm. Please don't
   try this at home!

10. Farmer's lung. Joe once fell in love with Patience,
    an American guest who was staying at Grey
    Gables. He wanted to join her in California, so he
    made a compensation claim for his farmer's lung
    to fund the trip. His claim was unsuccessful.

11. A telegram from the Queen, a pub in Hollerton.
    Eddie and Alf had visited the pub during their
    search for 'Carmen', the co-creator of Joe's
    mysterious hangover cure. They accidentally
    ended up in the audience for Carmen Avago,
    a drag queen cabaret act. After the show, the
    performer explained that the person they were
    looking for was, in fact, his mum. Joe had
    promised to share his wealth with her if the
    hangover cure ever took off. It didn't.

12. 'Some Day My Prince Will Come'. She was feeling blue as her relationship with Eddie didn't seem to be going anywhere.

13. An axe, stuck in his head. It wasn't put there by his younger brother Ed – it was only a prop!

14. William. He proposed on her nineteenth birthday.

15. Side A was 'Lambs to the Slaughter' and side B was 'Clarrie's Song'.

16. Jazzer McCreary. He's always had a way with words.

17. With a heavy heart, Clarrie locked the door as Joe couldn't bear to do it. They had fallen into dire financial straits and were declared bankrupt. The Grundys lost their tenancy of Grange Farm, which was sold to Oliver Sterling. When he went to Tuscany in 2015, Oliver allowed the Grundys to move back into Grange Farm temporarily; they've been there ever since.

18. Poppy.

19. The level of membership of the Grange Farm Cider Club. Joe invented the platinum

membership to buy Jim's silence when he discovered the Grundys were selling Tumble Tussock cider without a licence. It entitled him to a lifetime's free membership and he was relieved of all apple-picking duties. Bert was offered a gold membership for just £10, which entitled him to a yearly bottle of Tumble Tussock.

20. The last two words are 'life depart'.

The Dower House

1. Gin making.

2. An abattoir. After the local abattoir went into administration, Justin Elliott found himself in a bidding war with Vince Casey, the owner of a meat company. Several Ambridge farmers, including David Archer and Brian Aldridge, had been ripped off by Vince Casey in the past so keenly supported Justin. Vince ended up winning the bid, and to add insult to injury, David discovered that Justin had always planned to turn the abattoir into office space.

3. She's a dog.

4. Caroline and Lilian.

5. Botox injections.

6. The product was fictitious. Lipoflora is an anagram of April Fool and was invented by Lilian's brother Tony Archer and his wife Pat who were playing a prank on her.

7. Matt Crawford. His inflated ego and balding head clearly didn't put Lilian off though; the two of them were an item, on and off, for over a decade.

8. Mike was teaching Lilian how to do ballroom dancing. Lilian was mortified to discover Matt avoided dancing with her because he thought she had two left feet. She secretly employed Mike to help polish her cha-cha.

9. Wellies.

10. Paul, Matt's half-brother, said this to Lilian, at the end of their affair. They rekindled their illicit relationship a couple of years later until Paul died of a heart attack.

11. Lingerie. It was in fact pieces of pottery.

12. Husband Lester 'Nick' Nicholson, a Royal Canadian Air Force officer, had a fall after sleepwalking. He was in hospital at the time with an ear condition. They had been married for less than a year.

13. Cameron Fraser, who vanished to escape his creditors.

14. Greg Turner, the gamekeeper. Matt used to make Greg's life a misery over the organisation of the shoot.

15. Mrs Beard, the nanny Lilian employed to look after James.

16. Amside Property Holdings, which Lilian still owns. Lilian's properties were all she was left with when Matt absconded to Costa Rica.

17. Mrs Blossom.

18. Lilian Archer, who became Mrs Ralph Bellamy in the year 1970. The World Cup finals were held that year in Mexico.

19. Venice. Lilian and Ralph Bellamy honeymooned there and Gilbert and Sullivan's *The Gondoliers* uses it as a setting.

20. LILIAN is worth 17. IAN = 6, i.e. 1 + 2 + 3 in no particular order, therefore L must be greater than 3. It cannot be greater than 4, or the total value of ALAN would be higher than 8. L = 4 so A + A + N also = 4. A = 1, N = 2. I must = 3.

Reflections:
All Creatures Great and Small

1. Scruff gin. It was Robert Snell's suggestion to honour his and Lynda's beloved pet.

2. Lynda's llamas. They were named after Mozart and his wife.

3. Capricorn, the goat. Both of them were born in early January.

4. Wolf-whistle. Joe found his feathered friend while out walking one day. He made sure Basil felt right at home, even going so far as to bathe him in the bathroom basin using Clarrie's flannel and towel. The happy partnership eventually came to an end when Joe took Basil to a big parrot show, where he was spotted and reclaimed by his rightful owner.

5. *Mother Goose.*

6. Red. Red Link and Red Knight.

7. Goats owned by Lynda Snell.

8. A cup of tea.

9. Captain. He was Jack Woolley's Staffordshire bull terrier.

10. Nightingale Farm.

11. Barbarella. She was a Berkshire sow whom Eddie affectionately nicknamed 'Miss Babs'.

12. Borsetshire Beauties are cider apples. Toby once fed Rex's boar, Basil, half a sack of fermenting apples, leaving the pig as drunk as a skunk.

13. Romeo – though Eddie's cultural reference point was the Beckham family; he had another called Brooklyn!

14. Geese. The Grundys are famed for their turkeys.

15. They were the front and rear of the pantomime cow. The year was 2008 and the panto was *Jack and the Beanstalk*.

16. As leader of the Ambridge Palm Sunday service. Benjamin is Shula's donkey. Although he's usually impeccably behaved, in one service he took a fancy to Pat Fletcher's hat,

which he attempted to eat in front of the congregation.

17. Pigs. Neil Carter's animals had escaped. Eddie Grundy, who happened to be passing, selflessly offered to remove the pigs. For a modest fee, of course.

18. Brookfield.

19. Animal passports. Eddie even faked a letter from the Ministry of Agriculture, Fisheries and Food to convince Joe.

20. A tarantula. Much to Jim's annoyance, Jazzer insisted on keeping his 'darling' Webster in the living room.

The Am

1. The Aldridges. Chemicals had been illegally disposed of forty years previously and compensation had to be paid out.

2. South.

3. The bridge is haunted, according to one of Joe's ghost stories. His Uncle Enoch saw the ghost of a murdered shepherd once. There was a warning that you should never cross the narrow bridge out of Ambridge, lest you see his ghost. If you saw him, it meant danger was coming.

4. The Perch.

5. Four.

6. Once called The Bull Upstairs, the function room was renamed the Flood Bar. Even after the main pub reopened its doors, the Flood Bar retained its name.

7. A karaoke night.

8.   Kirsty Miller. She was taking an invigorating swim which led to the discovery of numerous dead fish.

9.   Slurry. It leaked from Brookfield into the Am.

10. An otter. A Mrs Mitchell reported the discovery to the *Borchester Echo*.

11. Adam Macy. Adam and Ian had a bucket list to mark their final months as a duo before the birth of their son. Kate collected challenges from each of the family members, which the couple had to pull out of a hat. Kate challenged them to skinny-dip in the Am, but they were concerned that Jazzer might get quite a shock on his milk round.

12. Alan Franks. Sadly Freda did not make a full recovery and passed away at Borchester General Hospital.

13. George Barford. The memorial bridge was thought to be a more fitting tribute to such an integral member of the community than a stile or bench.

14. The Bull and Bluebell Cottage. Nightingale Farm is the one that does back on to the Am.

15. David Archer. When David was reported missing, the police assumed he was sleeping off a hangover somewhere, but instead he was conducting a heroic rescue.

16. Her golden jubilee, 2002.

17. The Stables. Rob took the Arkwright Lake boat to reach them.

18. Bra. The river was originally called the Ambra.

19. Trout. Schubert wrote the *Trout Quintet*, HMS *Troutbridge* was the ship in *The Navy Lark* and 2000 brown and rainbow trout were reintroduced to the Am.

20. Joe Grundy's ghost walk. It was held on Friday, 31 October 2008. The tickets cost £10 to include refreshments of hot home-made soup and cider.

Brookfield

1. A sheep (a ewe). Dan's last words were to Elizabeth, he told her to be a good girl.

2. Philip (Phil) Archer. He was David's father, and Pip's grandfather. She is Philippa, known as Pip.

3. Kirsty Miller and Philip Moss. It was due to be more than an engagement party, as they were planning to announce that they had already married.

4. David Archer, because he had very blond hair like his mum, Jill.

5. Jill and Leonard. The car was bright orange and Roy Tucker likened it to a motorised tangerine.

6. It was a stunt bottom, for the notoriously bawdy 'The Miller's Tale'. Ben made a replacement out of papier mâché. This came as a relief to the cast as Lynda's back-up option had been using Nathan Booth as a body double.

7. He sold his antiques business. Kenton renamed it Archers Antiquities and ran it for five years.

8. A glass of red wine. They were at Nelson's Wine Bar when Robin told Elizabeth he wanted to remain with his wife and save his marriage.

9. Marmalade. Phil wisely finally decided that his wife's marmalade was superior to Heather's.

10. Spaghetti Bolognese. He enlisted Pip to help with the cooking and had a great night joking around with the children while Ruth tearfully ended her affair outside a hotel in Oxford.

11. Elizabeth. The farm was ultimately left to David and Ruth, with the other siblings getting a share of the proceeds if it was ever sold.

12. It was due to the outbreak of foot-and-mouth disease.

13. Nightingale Farm. Ruth moved out when she went to study at Harper Adams, and then she and David returned as newly-weds. They had to sleep on the floor for a while as their landlady's dog gave birth to puppies on their bed.

14. The wedding of Prince Andrew and Sarah Ferguson. David and Sophie were due to marry

in Felpersham Cathedral the following year, but they called the engagement off.

15. It was the music her ice cream van played. She had a student job and her rival in the cornet wars was Nigel Pargetter. His van played the 'Teddy Bears' Picnic'.

16. A barn. It had been set on fire deliberately and was being reduced to ashes.

17. Jude, from 'Hey Jude'. He was her unsuitable older boyfriend who unceremoniously ditched her to travel round America.

18. Ben.

19. East Field and West Field. The odds are one in six.

20. Edward Thomas. Kenton is Kenton Edward Archer. His younger brother is David Thomas Archer.

Bridge Farm

1. Tony and Pat Archer.

2. £1 million.

3. No it isn't!

4. The milking parlour. Tom discovered him lying on the floor in agony.

5. Always one to invest wisely, it was Jazzer McCreary. His eight-legged friend is called Webster.

6. Roy Tucker.

7. Dairy cattle. They are an attractive red pied breed called Montbéliardes.

8. A prize bull.

9. The death of her brother John and the suicide of her partner Greg led to Helen's illness.

10. No. The year was 1974. She had thought Tony

was about to propose to her, but he instead brought up the subject of culling a cow. Pat took matters into her own hands and told him she was worried they were going to spend the rest of their lives talking about cows. If Tony wouldn't get round to asking her, she'd do it instead: would he marry her? They became Mr and Mrs Archer within two months.

11. A caravan.

12. Mike Tucker. He already had a milk round covering the area.

13. Ambridge Organics.

14. An MG Midget. Tony has always loved his sports cars. Beechwood resident Joy Horville also owns an MG Midget and the two bonded over their car choice. Tony spent so much time tinkering under Joy's bonnet that Tom suspected they were more than just friends. In 2019, he ruined Christmas lunch at Bridge Farm by wrongly accusing Tony and Joy of having an affair.

15. The *Guardian*. Tony was furious.

16. He proposed marriage to Hayley Jordan. Despite

still loving John, Hayley declined because she couldn't forgive his infidelity with Sharon.

17. Cheese. It's always proved popular, despite a lapse in production during a TB outbreak, and is said to go well in a sandwich.

18. 1984.

19. Superman.

20. It was a Ferguson tractor (a Fergie) which caused the death of their elder son John.

Reflections:
What's Your Emergency?

1. Helen stabbing Rob at Blossom Hill Cottage. The case even made it into the national press: the tabloids used a crazed-looking photo of Helen from her starring role in *Blithe Spirit*, whereas Rob was depicted with a wholesome photo from the village 'Clean for the Queen' event.

2. It was one of Jill's homemade flapjacks – ironically she was protesting against food waste at the Duxford sisters' restaurants.

3. His neck. Rex played second row professionally. He used to joke that rugby was their family business as his brother Toby was also a keen sportsman.

4. She confessed to Joe that she was the person who knocked Matt Crawford down in a hit-and-run accident.

5. Wayne Tucson, Jill Archer, then Freddie Pargetter.

6. Attempting to pervert the course of justice. She had harboured her wayward brother, Clive Horrobin. He escaped from prison after being charged for raiding the village shop.

7. Nigel and Freddie Pargetter. Nigel was riding a quad bike in 2002. Freddie was riding a horse in 2012.

8. They were there to welcome him home after his spell in prison following the death of Bob Larkin.

9. Simon Pemberton.

10. On a whisky bottle. Nelson Gabriel and Charles Brown stole the van, and despite Nelson's incriminating fingerprints, he was acquitted.

11. Elizabeth Archer. The vandal was her ex-boyfriend Tim Beecham. It was particularly embarrassing as her father, Phil Archer, was a magistrate at the time.

12. Jill – it's a thyroid deficiency.

13. Jennifer Archer. The year was 1967 and that summer she gave birth to Adam.

14. Adam Macy. Adam was so badly assaulted that he had to be placed in intensive care. Keith Horrobin and his gang were responsible for the attack.

15. The single wicket.

16. The WI – his talk, all about home security, commanded a considerably larger turnout than normal.

17. Matt Crawford. He had been hoping to persuade Lilian to run away with him, and when she didn't return his calls he decided to walk to Grey Gables to profess his love to her.

18. Bonfire Night, 5 November. Joe reckoned the fireworks masked the sound of gunfire.

19. Sorry Pusscat. This was his nickname for Lilian.

20. She let down the tyres of the getaway van.

Home Farm

1. Spiritual Home.

2. The purchase of Home Farm. This was in 1975 and he married Jennifer a year later in 1976 in an uncharacteristically modest ceremony at Borchester Register Office.

3. He invested in a farm in Hungary.

4. Winston Churchill. Jazzer said little Xander looked like 'Winston Churchill having a burp'. This was a sentiment echoed by Eddie Grundy some thirty years earlier on seeing baby Chris Carter, when he said, 'All babies look like Winston Churchill.'

5. Gills. Fish breathe through gills, a gill is an imperial measure and a gill is a wooded ravine. The Gill family moved into Home Farm after the Aldridges were forced to move on.

6. Adam. Sensing that Adam wasn't keen on taking things further after their one-night stand in a hotel, Pawel then made a move on Ian!

7. Caroline Bone. After his tryst with Caroline, he had a flirtation with Mandy Beesborough of the Pony Club. Brian notoriously took Mandy and friends to the races on the day that Jennifer was giving birth to Alice. His final, most serious affair was with Siobhan Hathaway, with whom he had a child.

8. Macy-Craig.

9. Raddle powder (sheep dye).

10. They were both Irish. Paddy Redmond was the father of Adam and Siobhan Hathaway was the mother of Ruairi.

11. Ed was delivering illegal chemicals at night. In a desperate bid to earn more money towards his first home, Ed accepted some odd jobs off a man named Tim Oatey, but before long he was embroiled in dodgy chemical deliveries.

12. Betty Tucker (Betty declined the offer).

13. Ian Craig. It's an anagram. It was a ruse to have a meeting with Adam.

14. A polytunnel. It was the only place they could find privacy after their dates kept being interrupted by family and friends.

15. Jill (Archer) and Jennifer (Aldridge).

16. Robert Snell. Brian was burning off stubble from a crop he only planted so he could claim a subsidy for it.

17. Shepherd's pie. He was in charge of the Home Farm flock.

18. A handkerchief that his mother Siobhan dropped, which belonged to her stepfather Brian, and had his monogram on it. She also noticed an uncanny resemblance between Ruairi and a baby photo of Alice.

19. Trichloroethylene is sometimes known as Tricky, and is the chemical that polluted the Am and forced Brian and Jennifer to leave their beloved Home Farm.

20. The mazes at Home Farm. Each year the maze had a particular theme. The mazes were formed in fields of maize, leading to some awful puns!

Willow Farm and Ambridge Hall

1. Goose. This was very popular in Victorian times.

2. Ed and Emma.

3. Coriander. She used to shorten it to 'Caz'.

4. The Snell's dog, Scruff.

5. The Dower House.

6. Bobby Bodger. His nickname for Lynda was Lyndybottom!

7. Elizabeth Pargetter (née Archer). Not only did it cost Roy his marriage, he also walked out on his job at Lower Loxley, where Elizabeth was his boss.

8. Feng shui. Her boss, Caroline, told Lynda in no uncertain terms that her obsession with the practice had to stop when she started rearranging all the furniture at Grey Gables too.

9. She was a dental nurse. Mr Bubbles was the nickname. It was also the name of Vicky's favourite teddy bear.

10. Francis Winterbury is Ambridge's MP. Lynda is a keen letter writer, and quick to highlight issues in the local area. She even wrote to the local MP about flood defences on the Am (though clearly without much luck . . .).

11. Phoebe. Jennifer was distraught at having to move from a manor house to a semi-detached cottage with a mere two bedrooms.

12. Dame Edna Everage. Each grande dame felt they got the better of the other.

13. Village doctor.

14. William Shakespeare.

15. Willow Cottage was created. Mike extended and divided the original farmhouse to create a cottage for Roy, Hayley and the children to live in next door.

16. The Cat and Fiddle public house. The inn had closed down, but ultimately Matt Crawford and

Stephen Chalkman had it converted into swanky modern apartments.

17. Lord Robert Winston. The following year, Hayley gave birth to baby Abbie.

18. Seven. It's always been Lynda's lucky number. It's the fourth prime number, after two, three and five. It proved to be extra lucky in her Christmas production of *Snow White and the Seven Dwarfs*, which was a roaring success.

19. The musician in question was Salieri, a rival of Mozart. One of Lynda's llamas had the same name.

20. Cricket umpiring. She became something of an expert in the laws of cricket after swotting up on them for the Beat the Brainboxes quiz at The Bull.

Grey Gables and
The Lodge

1. The kitchen. A workman had been using the grill to make a sandwich, while lifting the floor tiles with petrol.

2. Royal. For a while, Caroline called the Royal Garden Suite home while she worked at Grey Gables. The luxurious accommodation was offered to her as an incentive not to quit her job.

3. Hazel.

4. Conference room.

5. A golf course. The course has gone through a lot in its time: it was turfed up when the hunt gave chase across it; vandalised by Ambridge treasure hunters; flooded; and even closed during the foot-and-mouth outbreak, yet it's still going strong.

6. The cake. Made by Clarrie, the top tier of the cake was destroyed when Caroline slipped on a wet floor and landed on it. Ian didn't have time to replace the fruit cake and hurriedly made and

iced a Victoria sponge instead. Thankfully no one noticed the substitution.

7.   Raspberry coulis. A blender had exploded, spreading its contents all over the face of one of the Grey Gables' chefs.

8.   She complained her room was haunted.

9.   She had a fall, tripping over Peggy's cat Hilda, and moved to The Laurels, initially as a temporary measure.

10. The Cider Club, operating out of Grange Farm.

11. Joe Grundy. Well, he would, wouldn't he?

12. The horse was called Midnight. Grace had gone outside to look for an earring which she had mislaid.

13. He was Jack's chauffeur. As well as being a gardener and general handyman, Higgs drove Jack's Bentley for thirty years.

14. Grey Silk. It was a racehorse given to him in lieu of money owed.

15. Princess Margaret.

16. The hotel dog, Captain, ate the cake.

17. Radio 1. The legendary John Peel attended.

18. Pemberton (when she was married to Guy). Her other names were Bone and Sterling.

19. The sound of fireworks on Bonfire Night. Jack always loved Bonfire Night, but his Alzheimer's left him increasingly confused.

20. The golf course, after the COVID-19 restrictions were lifted.

Reflections:
What's in a Name?

1. Nelson (Gabriel).

2. The name Eccles. Eccles was the peacock who resided at The Bull for many years before Kenton ran him over. An Eccles cake is a flaky pastry containing currants. Eccles is a town in Greater Manchester. Eccles, voiced by Spike Milligan, was a not-too-bright character in the radio comedy *The Goons*.

3. Lynda Snell, who wrote reviews for various local publications using an anagram of her own name as a nom de plume. She adopted her alter ego when she realised the editor of *Borsetshire Life* had blacklisted her work as 'Lynda Snell', and even created an email address in Dylan's name.

4. A field at Bridge Farm.

5. Casa Nueva, meaning 'new house'.

6. Greenwood Cottage. Will once again took inspiration from his honeymoon location, this

time 'Cape Verde', as verde is Portuguese for green.

7. PAT. Anagrams are APT and TAP.

8. They were both called Jack. She first married Jack Archer and then Jack Woolley.

9. Spinney.

10. Lexi. L = 50, X = 10 and I = 1.

11. Happy. The Happy Friends Café (a community venue run by volunteers) and Les Soeurs Heureuses (The Happy Sisters an upmarket, fine dining restaurant).

12. *Bunty.*

13. TOM.

14. Home Farm.

15. Ed and Emma (Grundy), and Tom and Pru (Forrest) with 6 letters each.

16. TONY. Add TONY to the words in capitals and you can make a square word box where the

words read the same both across and down.

DUET
UNDO
EDEN
TONY

17. A mode of transport is contained in each
     surname. Christopher CARter, Marjorie
     AntroBUS and Ruairi DonoVAN.

18. Alice Aldridge and Chris Carter, who married in
     Las Vegas. Brick was the name of the witness.
     Brian decided that for the sake of their sanity, he
     and Jennifer would have to view their daughter's
     wedding as her 'starter marriage'.

19. It is a cider apple.

20. 'Sweet Caroline', 'Pretty Amazing Grace' and
     'Cracklin' Rosie'. The prominent feature is of
     course the River Am in the title, 'I Am . . . I Said'.

The Cricket Pavilion and The Village Hall

1. Harrison Burns and Tracy Horrobin. Tracy triumphed by a single vote, but the outbreak of coronavirus meant no cricket could actually be played.

2. Neil Carter. He did, however, play King Clarence to Eddie's Queen Edwina. He wasn't impressed when Eddie started calling him 'Clarrie love'.

3. May.

4. Making cricket teas.

5. Joe Grundy. Lynda had her reservations as, when directing Joe, she felt one was lucky if he stumbled on stage with his pants the right way round. But her fears were unfounded and the production received rave reviews.

6. Tom Archer took the title role in *Robin Hood* in 2013.

7. She had used a professional gardener to help her. She's not the only villager whose actions have

caused a stir – in 2012, Jazzer was disqualified from the men-only bread-baking class for making his entry in a bread maker.

8. Anneka Rice.

9. They were pantomime characters in *Snow White and the Seven Dwarfs*; Kenton played Average and Edgar Titcombe was Shorty. All the dwarfs had height-related names.

10. Women were allowed to play.

11. The cricket pavilion was named after Jack Woolley, who had been a benefactor of the club for many years.

12. *Calendar Girls*.

13. The village school.

14. *A Christmas Carol*. Kathy was cast as the ghost of Christmas past. Lynda stepped in to play the role.

15. Susan Carter. Susan's position at the village shop has made her the eyes and ears of Ambridge, and she is usually the first to know about other people's business.

16. Clarrie Grundy.

17. A bowl of rice.

18. Freda Fry. She was a stalwart of the show and her floral offerings and culinary creations won her numerous prizes.

19. She directed *Blithe Spirit* by Noel Coward. She would have avoided his play *Hay Fever*, as she is a constant sufferer of this complaint.

20. The Felpersham Light Operatic Society.

Blossom Hill Cottage

1. Two.

2. Thatch.

3. Usha Franks.

4. She was Helen's defence counsel. Anna is a high-flying feminist barrister who specialises in domestic abuse cases.

5. The kitchen. After years of abuse, Helen finally snapped when Rob dared her to kill herself and tried to harm her son, Henry.

6. Attempted murder. She was acquitted on appeal.

7. He said he was going to send Henry away to boarding school.

8. Hitting Helen. At the time Rob told Helen she had given him no option but to hit her and convinced her that she needed psychiatric help.

9. Kirsty Miller. Helen phoned her in a frenzy thinking she had killed Rob, so Kirsty came straight round to investigate.

10. She had had a minor car accident.

11. Custard. Rob told Helen to make custard from scratch for his pudding, as he refused to eat 'shop-bought muck'.

12. Manor Court. Much to Carol's annoyance, John used this imposing eighteenth-century gentleman's house as a display centre for his antiques.

13. Blossom Hill Cottage had no electricity.

14. The cottage had been damaged by fire. She was accompanied to Home Farm by her cat Sammy, whom Brian loathed.

15. The spurned Usha had already sent all his furniture to a charity shop.

16. A weekend retreat for themselves. They spent weekdays living above a book shop in Borchester with Jennifer's son, Adam.

17. Jim Lloyd. He lived there before deciding to reside in Ambridge permanently, at which point he bought Greenacres.

18. Patrick Hamilton wrote a play called *Gaslight*, which was about coercive control and physical and mental abuse in the Victorian era. 'Gaslighting' describes the ordeal suffered by Helen at the hands of her husband Rob Titchener.

19. The Scombridae family is a family of fish, which includes the Thunnini group or tuna. Using up what little food there was in the house, Helen cooked Rob a tuna pasta bake on the night of the stabbing. He'd previously told her he loathed tuna, but on this evening he polished off the whole meal, saying it was one of the tastiest things she'd ever cooked. When questioned on his change of heart, Rob tried to convince Helen she was imagining things. He was exercising coercive control.

20. The plumber. Jennifer Archer was one of several teachers. Anisha Jayakody was a veterinary surgeon. Usha Gupta was the solicitor. Mike Daly was the spy. Jim Lloyd was the university professor.

Lower Loxley

1. David Archer. It was a bitterly cold, windy evening and the pair had decided to remove a banner from the roof.

2. The apple. Previous unmissable attractions have included pin the maggot on the apple, apple and spoon race, guess the apple variety and a longest peel competition.

3. Rare breed hens.

4. Therapist. She helped Elizabeth Pargetter to overcome her depression in 2019.

5. Bird seed.

6. A grape. It is an early ripening white grape from France's Loire Valley. It helped Nigel produce the Lower Loxley wine.

7. The alcohol licence, which had been revoked.

8. Mr Darcy in *Pride and Prejudice*.

9. Geri Halliwell, Ginger Spice. Harrison was wearing a copy of her famous Union Jack dress as a costume for his stag night.

10. The tutor, Russ Jones, was wearing a leather jacket that Freddie had previously seen left behind in the car he shares with Lily.

11. They had already booked a Gorillagram.

12. Cranford Crystal was the horse leading the hay wagon which bore Nigel's coffin to the Pargetter family church at Loxley Barratt.

13. A trowel. It reflects their history as plasterers.

14. Eat naughty children. She clearly wasn't a Mary Poppins kind of nanny!

15. Three pairs of her knickers! They sported the letter N, a heart shape and a letter E. This was of course the result of a prank involving Nigel and Kenton and while Elizabeth was deeply unimpressed, the bank managers found it hilarious.

16. *A Midsummer Night's Dream.* Nigel was playing Oberon, Elizabeth was Titania and Joe played Bottom.

17. Happy New Year.

18. Meredith. Bunbury was a fictitious person, invented as an alibi. Lily invented Meredith for the same reason, as she wished to hide an illicit affair. Freddie did nothing to correct Elizabeth when she got the wrong impression and thought Lily and 'Meredith' were in a relationship.

19. Snowy. Nigel sold ice cream as Mr Snowy and Tintin travels the world accompanied by Snowy the dog.

20. Lily and Freddie and Kenton and Shula are both sets of twins.

Reflections:
None of Your Business

1. Fruit drinks, though she previously worked in cosmetics. Natasha retained a lot of the knowledge from her former career and was roped into giving villagers makeovers for the 2019 Lent appeal.

2. Eggs. Josh used to work in partnership with Neil as a part-owner of his egg business, but he thought there was a quick buck to be made by buying into the Fairbrothers' Upper Class Eggs business too. Neil was less than impressed to discover that Josh had not only been poaching his customers, he'd also stolen a number of Neil's hens for the rival business too!

3. 'Worse than *The Apprentice*'.

4. She was the first female priest at St Stephen's, where she held the position for seven years.

5. Emma Grundy. She wanted to raise as much money as possible to put towards a home of her own on the Beechwood estate.

6. Fallon Rogers.

7. Jennifer Aldridge. She had honed her journalistic
    skills over many years as a reporter for the
    Borchester Echo and decided to pick up her
    pen again in 2019. The column has never
    changed its name, so Jennifer is the fifth 'Wendy'
    for the *Westbury Courier.*

8. They were vicars.

9. a) Richard, b) Leonard and c) Jim.

10. Baking. In 2006, Phil and Jill competed against
    one another in the 'green food' class of
    the Flower and Produce Show, Jill using
    food colouring and Phil using hemp flour.
    Jill's was highly commended while Phil
    didn't win anything – though Jazzer was
    very keen to place a bid on Phil's cake in the
    auction!

11. Gourmet Grills.

12. They have all been fortune tellers.

13. Well, no – you'd almost be right if you said
    David Archer or Tony Archer. Although David

was living at Brookfield when Britain joined the Common Market he was still at school at the time. Tony Archer was farming in Ambridge in 1973, but he didn't own his own farm.

14. It was a company with Matt Crawford as a director. Chalkman Crawford Capital Partners Limited was the full name. Whilst director of C3PL, Matt fraudulently persuaded the bank to loan the company £5 million. He was fined £1.6 million and given a prison sentence.

15. Medicine. He was the local GP whose marriage broke down after Siobhan's affair with Brian. He later married the vicar, Janet Fisher, and the pair left Ambridge.

16. About twenty years. Russ was the deputy principal of the college and lectured in art. Lily met him when she asked him for advice on the Gwen John painting she inherited from her father.

17. Eddie Grundy. He was talking to an auctioneer's agent who was cataloguing items to be sold off at Grange Farm before the family were evicted.

18. Police officer.

19. Jolene Archer.

20. They were estate agents. Shula worked there for
     twenty years.

THE ARCHERS TIMELINE – SEVENTY YEARS

1950s

1951   ~   The Archer family toast the new year. Dan, Doris, their children Jack, Phil and Christine, Jack's wife Peggy and Phil's girlfriend Grace Fairbrother all gather together at Brookfield to bid farewell to the year 1950.

      ~   Peggy gives birth to Anthony (Tony), her third child.

1952   ~   Jack Archer applies to be licensee of The Bull.

1954   ~   Dan buys Brookfield farm from Squire Lawson-Hope.

      ~   Jack spends several months in hospital, struggling with alcoholism and depression.

      ~   Phil proposes to Grace.

1955   ~   Phil and Grace marry.

      ~   Grace dies after a shocking fire.

1956 ~ Foot-and-mouth disease strikes Brookfield.

     ~ Christine Archer marries Paul Johnson.

1957 ~ Tom Forrest is tried, and acquitted, for manslaughter after killing Bob Larkin in a struggle.

     ~ Phil takes on a farm he names Hollowtree and sets up a pig unit.

1958 ~ Jill gives birth to Kenton and Shula.

1959 ~ Jack and Peggy Archer buy The Bull.

     ~ Jill gives birth to David.

1960s

1962 ~ Birmingham businessman Jack Woolley buys Grey Gables.

1965 ~ Christine and Paul adopt a son called Peter.

1966 ~ Jennifer (then Archer) discovers she's pregnant.

1967 ~ Carole Grenville marries John Tregorran and the pair move into Manor Court.

     ~ Jill gives birth to Elizabeth.

~ Jennifer gives birth to her illegitimate son, Adam.

1968 ~ Jennifer marries Roger Travers-Macy.

1969 ~ Lilian Archer marries Canadian airman Lester 'Nick' Nicholson.

~ Dan retires. He and Doris move to Glebe Cottage while Phil, Jill and the children move to Brookfield.

1970s

1970 ~ Lilian's husband dies unexpectedly.

~ Jennifer gives birth to Deborah (Debbie) on Christmas Eve.

1971 ~ Lilian marries the wealthy Ralph Bellamy.

1972 ~ Jack Archer succumbs to alcoholism, dying aged forty-nine.

1974 ~ Kenton enrols in the Merchant Navy.

~ Tony Archer marries Pat Lewis.

1975 ~ Lilian and Ralph move away to Guernsey.

 ~ Joe Grundy sends shockwaves through the village when he hosts a pop concert on his land.

 ~ Pat gives birth to John Archer.

1976 ~ Jennifer marries Brian Aldridge and moves to Home Farm.

1977 ~ Jennifer Aldridge gives birth to Katherine (Kate).

1978 ~ Pat and Tony take over the Bridge Farm tenancy.

 ~ The Grundys start their turkey-rearing business.

 ~ Christine's husband Paul is killed in Germany. She agrees to marry George Barford.

1979 ~ Pat gives birth to Helen Archer.

1980s

1980   ~   Ralph Bellamy dies, leaving Lilian a wealthy widow.

    ~   Doris Archer dies peacefully at home.

1981   ~   Pat gives birth to Thomas (Tom) Archer.

    ~   Eddie Grundy marries Clarrie Larkin.

1982   ~   Polly Perks dies in a tragic accident.

1983   ~   Clarrie Grundy gives birth to William (Will).

1984   ~   Neil Carter marries Susan Horrobin. She gives birth to Emma.

    ~   HRH Princess Margaret visits Ambridge.

    ~   Clarrie Grundy gives birth to Edward (Ed).

1985   ~   Shula marries Mark Hebden.

1986   ~   Dan Archer dies.

    ~   Robert and Lynda Snell move to Ambridge.

1988   ~   Jennifer Aldridge gives birth to Alice.

    ~   David Archer marries agricultural student Ruth Pritchard.

1989 ~ Brian Aldridge suffers post-traumatic epilepsy after being charged by a cow.

1990s

1992 ~ Elizabeth has an abortion after Cameron Fraser abandons her.

1993 ~ Ruth and David's first child, Philippa (Pip), is born.

   ~ Clive Horrobin robs the village shop at gunpoint, embroiling sister Susan Carter in his criminal activity.

1994 ~ Mark Hebden dies in a car accident. His and Shula's much-longed-for son Daniel is born later that year.

   ~ Nigel Pargetter marries Elizabeth Archer.

1995 ~ Usha Gupta is targeted in a series of racist attacks.

   ~ Caroline Bone marries estate owner Guy Pemberton.

1996 ~ The three local parishes merge, bringing a woman vicar to Ambridge.

1997 ~ Ruth gives birth to Joshua (Josh).

1998 ~ John Archer dies in a tractor accident.

~ Nelson Gabriel puzzles villagers and creditors alike by disappearing.

~ Kate Aldridge gives birth to Phoebe, daughter of Roy Tucker.

~ Alistair Lloyd and Shula Hebden marry on Christmas Eve.

1999 ~ Elizabeth Pargetter gives birth to Lily and Frederick (Freddie).

2000s

2000 ~ The Grundys are evicted from Grange Farm.

~ Ruth is diagnosed with breast cancer.

~ Sid and Kathy Perks divorce.

2001 ~ Brookfield goes into lockdown during a foot-and-mouth outbreak.

~ Shula and Alistair buy The Stables from Christine.

~ Kate gives birth to Noluthando and moves

out to South Africa, where she marries Lucas Madikane.

~ Nelson Gabriel dies in Argentina.

~ Emma Carter and Ed Grundy have a serious car accident.

2002 ~ Ruth gives birth to Benjamin (Ben).

~ Gamekeeper Greg Turner takes his own life.

~ Siobhan Hathaway gives birth to a son, Ruairi. Brian Aldridge is his father.

2004 ~ William Grundy marries Emma Carter.

2005 ~ Emma Grundy gives birth to baby George. There is a paternity battle between her husband Will and his brother Ed.

~ Betty Tucker dies.

2006 ~ Ruth has an affair with Sam Batton, but ends it, deciding to rescue her marriage with David.

~ Adam Macy and Ian Craig enter into a civil partnership.

2007 ~ Siobhan Hathaway dies. Jennifer agrees to bring up Brian's son, Ruairi.

2008 ~ Alan Franks and Usha Gupta marry.

~ Pat and Tony buy the freehold for Bridge Farm.

2009 ~ Mike Tucker marries Vicky Hudson
after a whirlwind romance.

~ Matt Crawford is imprisoned for fraud.

2010s

2010 ~ Phil Archer dies.

~ Sid Perks dies in New Zealand.

~ Christopher Carter and Alice Aldridge marry
in Las Vegas.

~ Kate returns from South Africa.

2011 ~ Nigel Pargetter falls from the roof of Lower
Loxley to his death.

~ Helen Archer gives birth to Henry.

2012 ~ Will Grundy marries Nicola (Nic) Hanson.

~ Tony Archer has a heart attack, but
recovers.

2013 ~ Will and Nic's daughter Poppy is born.

2014 ~ Jack Woolley dies.

~ Tom Archer jilts Kirsty Miller on their wedding day.

~ Roy Tucker and Elizabeth Pargetter have an affair, ending Roy's marriage to Hayley (née Jordan).

~ Tony is trampled by a bull.

2015 ~ Ruth and David contemplate selling Brookfield and moving to Northumbria.

~ A flood tears through Ambridge, causing considerable damage to many homes.

~ Ed and Emma get married.

~ Helen Archer and Rob Titchener elope. They marry on the Isle of Wight.

2016 ~ Helen stabs Rob after suffering a period of abuse. She was sent to a women's prison, then moved to a mother and baby unit to give birth to her son Jack. Eventually she was acquitted.

~ Rob absconds to the USA.

2017 ~ Caroline Sterling dies in Tuscany.

~ Jill Archer is arrested for assault and released with a caution.

2018 ~ Nic Grundy dies of sepsis.

~ Pip Archer gives birth to Rosie after a fling with Toby Fairbrother.

~ Freddie is arrested for drug dealing and sentenced to six months in a young offender institution.

2019 ~ Brian pleads guilty to contaminating the Am. The family sell Home Farm.

~ Jill introduces her boyfriend Leonard Berry to the Archer family.

~ Tom Archer marries Natasha Thomas a week after proposing.

~ Alistair Lloyd discovers his father Jim was abused as a child.

~ Adam and Ian's son, Alexander Macy-Craig, is born.

~ Joe Grundy dies.

2020s

2020 ~ The Bull changes its name.

     ~ There is an explosion at Grey Gables. Lynda
Snell is severely injured but survives.

     ~ Ambridge goes into lockdown for COVID-19.

THE HISTORY
OF THE SHOW

'And a very Happy New Year to you all,' said Dan Archer on 1 January 1951. With those words, *The Archers* as we know it was born. After a successful pilot week on the BBC Midlands Home Service in the spring of the previous year, it was decided that the programme had a broad enough appeal to be broadcast nationwide. Godfrey Baseley, its creator, produced *The Archers* in response to farmers' wishes for 'a farming *Dick Barton*', so writers of the popular thriller series were drafted in to work on the programme. Though its original intention was to educate farmers trying to feed a post-war population, investment in the dramatic storylines is what has kept listeners tuning in for seven decades.

In 1955, one of the programme's most renowned events was aired, when the character Grace Fairbrother was killed after getting caught up in a fire. It was claimed to be a coincidence that this monumental event, which attracted 20 million listeners and caused the BBC switchboard to jam for two days, occurred on the same evening that ITV was launched...

In its seventy-year history, the programme's format has only undergone minor changes. Godfrey Baseley chose 'Barwick Green' as the programme's theme tune, and this toe-tapping melody has endured for seventy years. In 1964, episode repeats were introduced the afternoon after broadcast, and in 1998 five fifteen-minute episodes were replaced with six twelve-and-a-half-minute episodes per week. In 2004, *The Archers* moved from its home in Pebble Mill, Edgbaston, to studios in central Birmingham at The Mailbox, where it is still recorded. *The Archers* saw perhaps its greatest formatting change in 2020, when the programme came off air for the first time in seventy years. The nationwide lockdown which was implemented to try and contain the coronavirus pandemic meant that the cast and crew were unable to record episodes from the Birmingham studio. For three weeks, the programme came off air and was replaced by repeats of episodes from the archives. In this time, a new-style programme was written and devised, and actors recorded monologues from makeshift studios in their own homes. If *The Archers* can weather a global pandemic, it seems as though we can look forward to hearing the dulcet notes of 'Barwick Green' each evening for many years to come.

ACKNOWLEDGEMENTS

This book is a team effort, a coming together of five extraordinary mindsets. It was the idea of Alan Samson, the editor of Weidenfeld & Nicolson; it was a little something he and I cooked up over a delightful tea at the Langham Hotel opposite Broadcasting House in London; Roy and Sue Preston from Puzzle House have been truly ingenious quizmasters; Charlotte Davey, who has a peerless knowledge of *The Archers* which is ridiculous in someone so young, has mined the Ambridge archive to make sure we have got everything correct, and has furnished the answers with plentiful helpings of Ambridge arcana; Caroline Harrington, who has penned some of Lynda Snell's best put-downs over the many years she has scripted the show, has written the introductions. I thank them all, but most of all I should like to thank Carole Boyd, whose brilliant creation Lynda Snell is. I can think of no other character quite like Carole's Lynda Snell – she has been the inspiration for this book.

And in case you were wondering – the answer to the accumulator question is below.

Jeremy Howe

Accumulator answer:
HAPPY SEVENTIETH